Agenda for Prophets

AGENDA FOR PROPHETS

Towards a Political Theology for Britain

Edited by Rex Ambler and David Haslam

(Quaker)

THE BOWERDEAN PRESS 1980

First published in 1980 by
The Bowerdean Press
15 Blackfriars Lane
London EC4V 6ER

Designed by Douglas Martin

Printed and bound by
Billing and Sons Ltd
Guildford and Worcester

261.7

British Library Cataloguing in Publication Data:
Agenda for Prophets.
   1. Christianity and politics — Addresses, essays, lectures
   I. Ambler, Rex II. Haslam, David
   261.7'08   BR115.P7

   ISBN 0-906097-08-8
   ISBN 0-906097-09-6 Pbk

20029394

Contents

Dedication

Without the courage and commitment of Christians in many parts of the so-called 'underdeveloped world', particularly Latin America, this book would never have been written. They have studied and discussed, acted and been arrested, suffered imprisonment, torture and even death. They include priests, workers, theologians and students. In the engagement of Christian thought with Christian praxis they have created a new vision of the Kingdom and demonstrated to the Church in the West a fresh and exciting way of being Christians. In Theology, they have become the developed world and we the underdeveloped. To those who continue to blaze the trail and to those who have gone before this book is dedicated.

David Haslam
Rex Ambler
January 1980

'Would God that all the Lord's people were prophets.'

Moses, in *Numbers*, 11 v.29

Towards a Political Theology for Britain - An Introduction

David Haslam

'The Western Church has failed completely to prepare us for independence, both practically, in terms of a local trained leadership, and theologically, in terms of being able to relate Christianity to the creation of a socialist society;' the words of an African Christian leader in newly-independent Mozambique, bitterly critical of doctrinal nakedness before the Marx-inspired movements now holding the key to the future of southern Africa. 'The peculiarities of our language and our culture are stretched like a veil between Scripture and us; this keeps from us, the intended hearers, the biblical message which could challenge both our moral codes and our entire civilisation;' the sweeping denunciation by a Mexican theologian writing about the way Western theologians and exegetes have seriously misinterpreted the Bible's teaching on justice and salvation, in order to create and sustain — albeit unconsciously — a social system founded on injustice and exploitation. 'The Church? The Church has been responsible for the brain-washing, the mental slavery, of our people for the last 500 years. The fact that some Christians seem to be waking to that fact does not excuse the whole Christian religion from its part in the psychological, social and political oppression of black people;' the comments of a young black militant in a British city asked about the place of the Church in building a multiracial Britain.

In the midst of these 'external criticisms' of the theological condition of the West, in which Britain is obviously included, what kind of response is being made? What kind of theology is emerging in answer to such a questioning of the fundamental 'world-view' from which 'British theology' (if indeed there is such a thing) operates? The book to cause by far the biggest controversy in Britain over the last decade has been *The Myth of God Incarnate*,[1] which managed to spend a great deal of academic energy on what is admittedly an important Christian doctrine, but without even touching on the questions raised by comments such as those which open this introduction.

In a sense the whole 'Myth' debate, further fuelled by the conservative response 'The Truth of God Incarnate', is symbolic of what critics of Western theology are saying. 'Incarnation' for our theologians is a concept for theological debate, instead of being a challenge to revolutionary commitment. Yet 'Incarnation' is a revolutionary concept. A Cuban pastor visiting Britain interpreted its primary meaning as 'Solidarity', God in solidarity with us, thereby laying on us a demand for us to be in solidarity with our fellow human-beings in their pain, their loneliness, their hunger, their oppression. Not in many places did that kind of thinking penetrate into the 'Great Myth Debate'.

Questions like this are what has triggered off the search for a 'Political Theology'. Various definitions of this phrase have been offered. Linguistically speaking it clearly suggests a theology 'of the affairs of human society'. It may be argued that no theology could be otherwise. In fact the vast majority of theological thought concerns itself comparatively little with human affairs, despite the centrality of the Incarnation in Christian teaching. However, theology, even though claiming to be apolitical, always has political consequences. As Alistair Kee points out in the introduction to his first anthology of political theology,[2] 'For most of history theology has been biased towards the political right; nor was this challenged. Political theology is biased towards the left; why should it be challenged?' But we know why it is, because the interests of the socio-economic institution described as 'the Christian Church' lie, like every other social institution, in the maintenance of the status quo!

Political Theology is therefore seen as left-wing, and indeed it has been inspired in many cases by the stimulus of the Christian-Marxist dialogue. There are, however, two types of political theology, that which is 'reformist', in the sense of attempting to introduce a political dimension into the stream of Western liberal theology, and that which is genuinely radical, and wishes to begin from entirely different theological presuppositions altogether. The work of some of the 'liberation' theologians, such as Miranda, Bonino and Gutierrez, seems of a different dimension from even the most accomplished Western theology. Possibly it is the effect of being in a situation where one's theological commitment may involve imprisonment, torture and death. The most 'political' of Western theologians have never seriously had to face that kind of threat since the 1930s, in Germany. It is significant that then, amidst the rise of fascism, most European theologians were able to continue their 'theological' activities without any repercussions. A genuine 'political theology' is therefore by definition a threat to the status quo. That may be true in many supposedly 'socialist' countries as well as all the capitalist ones, and it is in line with the Biblical experience of the Prophets, John the Baptist, Jesus himself, and the Early Church.

Today's Church in Britain is about as far in class terms as you can get, except for certain small sects, from the earliest Christian communities. A Report to the National Methodist Conference in 1979 demonstrated that even Methodism, with its roots in the labour movement, was rapidly becoming an entirely middle-class Church. Political theology in its radical form is an attempt at theological class analysis and aims to rediscover the cutting edge, the 'skandalon' of the Gospel. There is hardly a sign of the 'skandalon' in the contemporary British ecclesiastical institution and as a result formal religion in Britain has nothing to say to the British people, except to serve, comfort and occasionally stimulate those whose class background coincides with the need for religious institutions.

In Kee's second anthology,[3] the contribution by Johannes Metz is part of his attack on 'The Privatisation of Religion'. Metz has been one of the prime movers in the West of the search for political theology and his statement that 'The deprivatising of theology is the primary critical task of political theology' sets our direction. The strongest dynamic has come, however, from beyond the confines of Western theology and it is a fundamental shift in the world of theology that the front line of theology today is not in the studies of Germany and the universities of the USA but in the favelas and prisons of Southern Africa, South East Asia and Latin America.

There have been a number of efforts to introduce onto the British theological scene the radical theology emanating from the 'Third World' – which includes the black communities of the USA and Britain as well as 95 per cent (the non-elite proportion) of the populations of Africa, Asia, Latin America and the Caribbean. Alistair Kee, as already mentioned, has made a particular contribution with his two volumes of selected essays and examples of political theological writing. They largely succeeded in their aims, both to inform and to whet appetites, but even among the snippets offered it was possible to distinguish the quite different perspectives from which 'First World' and 'Third World' theology are being written. Statements like this from Gutierrez, 'To know God is to do justice', strike at the heart of Western capitalist society and by implication at the institution of the Church, which has given capitalism its spiritual imprimatur for so long. The shortage of political analysis in the essays of the white Western theologians which are included – apart from committed activists such as Dan Berrigan – is symptomatic. The paucity of contributions from British sources is tragic. It is onto that somewhat empty stage that, diffidently, we have to try to move the scenery.

There are in fact some signs of activity backstage and some preparatory work to draw upon. There has been a short book from Mervyn Stockwood, Bishop of Southwark,[4] interpreting his understanding of the relationship

between Christianity and Marxism, and one from Lord Soper, giving a
rather early twentieth century view of 'Christianity and Politics'. There
have been two overviews, published in 1977 and 1978, of Church life in
Britain. There have been the beginnings of more cooperative theological
activities in sectors such as the inner cities (e.g. the Urban Theology Unit),
the women's movement (e.g. the Christian Parity Group) and industrial
mission (e.g. the Industrial Mission Association). In these perhaps lie the
greatest hope currently of progressive theological activity in Britain. Also
there have been one or two small books by notable personalities, inspired
by contacts with the world Church. Among these are included Pauline
Webb's *Salvation Today*,[5] arising from the international missionary
conference held in Bangkok in 1974 and reinterpreting the traditional
understanding of salvation in terms of Good News, and social justice, here
and now.

Ian Fraser's *The Fire Runs*[6] came from four years' experience as
coordinator of the World Council of Churches' programme 'Participation
in Change' and draws on his experiences in visiting widely differing
Christian communities. Colin Morris has continued to write essays and to
collect sermons in book form, but somehow the sharpness of his writing
out of the Zambian situation has become dulled and constrained after a
decade back in Britain. Derek Winter, a former Baptist missionary, who
revisited Brazil six years after a 14-year term there, recounts how he had
not recognised the fundamental political movement taking place on the
South American continent during his term and how his return there
inspired him with hope.[7] Sadly, though perhaps understandably, he makes
no attempt to relate his experience directly to a politics for Britain.
Finally, Bishop Colin Winter, who now calls himself a Namibian rather
than a Briton, and Cosmas Desmond, both long-time dwellers in the heat
and fire of the Southern African situation, have made contributions out of
their practical experiences which have much to say to the contemporary
British situation, if we have the ears to hear.[8,9]

The Bishop of Southwark's small book, *The Cross and the Sickle*,
illustrates the ever rosy view of the progressive churchman as to what
may be achieved by 'democratic means' in a society where the ruling
(assisted by the middle) classes not only control the means and finances of
production but also the media and, of course, the forces of law and order
too. Writes Stockwood: 'The fact is that a socialist economy is gradually
coming into existence as a consequence of parliamentary legislation.' The
problem of the so-called 'nationalised industries', who cut off gas and
electricity from the poorest, fail to provide a decent transport system to
low income communities and give large private companies preferential
discounts for their fuel supplies, may have escaped the Bishop but it has
not escaped those who live below the poverty line in Britain. One has to

listen hard and long to those from elsewhere who have participated in the
intense psychological and political struggle to create the beginnings of a
socialist society to understand the immense distance between 'mixed
economy' Britain and a truly socialist community. To the charge of
'Christian Marxist' the Bishop pleads guilty, though on a reading of this
book he need not do so. It is a further question as to whether the term
'Christian Marxist' makes sense at all. We shall return to that point a little
later.

The two overviews of the British Churches, *Change and the Churches*
by David Perman, subtitled 'An Anatomy of Religion in Britain', and
Trevor Beeson's *Britain Today and Tomorrow,* are descriptive rather than
analytical but nevertheless illustrate some of the problems facing the
attempt to develop a political theology for Britain.

Perman's book[10] looks at points of growth or controversy in the
Churches and includes chapters on Unity, the Charismatic Movement and
the Liturgical Revolution. Politics does finally make its entry and Perman
sees the British Churches as already 'deeply implicated' in political affairs,
particularly in the areas of education, Northern Ireland and race. However,
the lack of a politico-theological analysis in these areas is made even
clearer by Perman's account, which illustrates the nature of the failure of
the British Churches to address themselves to fundamental questions. For
example, there is more concern over the future of RE in schools than over
the failure to identify the underprivileged in our education system and to
develop a strategy for liberating them. He does better with Northern
Ireland, commenting on the British Churches' unwillingness to accept the
root causes of the poverty and the violence, and therefore to evolve real
hope of a solution. On race, Perman refers only to the Christian hysteria
surrounding the World Council of Churches' Programme to Combat
Racism's grants to Southern African liberation movements, while ignoring
racism at home. He himself points out the hypocrisy of British Church
posturing, both about the PCR and about racial issues within Britain itself.

Perman reveals his own position in the final paragraph of the book and
it is perhaps typical of apparently progressive church people in
contemporary Britain. 'At times, the leaders of opinion and action within
the Church will appear ... so intent on presenting to modern man a Gospel
that is reasonable, relevant and palatable that it is no longer the Gospel
but the policy strategy of a political party or a social work agency; there is
always the danger that the Kingdom of Heaven will become identified with
secular Utopias or political manifestos.' (p 228) Apart from the query as
to which 'church leaders' Perman is talking about, this kind of stated
position prompts a number of questions. Have those who adopt it studied
at any depth the Black and Liberation Theology of the 'Third World' or
taken seriously its implied fundamental criticisms of British Churches and

society? Secondly, why is it that, if the 'social (or political) Gospel provides such a 'reasonable and palatable' strategy, no political party or institutional Church body will come within a thousand miles of it? And thirdly, what is this 'Kingdom of Heaven' that is not to be identified with 'secular Utopias'? Better perhaps a 'secular Utopia' than the only stated alternative vision, which seems to consist largely of an ongoing eternal performance by the Mormon Tabernacle Choir, or its angelic equivalent. Such superficial posturing is rife among renewal-minded church people but it clearly will not do.

Trevor Beeson's *Britain Today and Tomorrow*[11] is the official summary of the British Council of Churches' project of the same name. The book's introduction recalls the Archbishop of Canterbury's 'Call to the Nation' and its question about what kind of society we want and what kind of people we need to be to achieve it. The lack of clarity in any answer to these questions, the Archbishop's own comments on a different occasion on the need to 'limit immigration' and the severe anxiety engendered in the religious (and daily) press by any attempt openly and rationally to discuss the possibility of genuine socialism in Britain demonstrate the enormous problems which faced Beeson. He tackles them courageously and at least takes seriously the dimensions of economics and politics which are so often conveniently ignored by ecclesiastical commentators. In the section on 'Education', church schools are relegated to the end of the chapter and the 'embattled position' of RE is hardly mentioned. There is, however, no attempt to offer any economic analysis and some of the basic political questions about our society fail to come out in a sufficiently sharp form. Perhaps this is inevitable in any document which endeavours to represent an even semi-official church position.

At the end of his last chapter, entitled 'For God's Sake Say Something', Beeson remarks: 'The cry of the world to the Churches of Britain and elsewhere is "For God's sake *do* something".' While that might be slightly overstating either the interest or the optimism of the rest of humanity in what the British Churches have to offer, in order to undertake any such action British Christians, like those in other parts of the world, will need a 'political theology'. *Britain Today and Tomorrow* paints the rather gloomy backcloth against which the drama must develop.

The work of some of the 'cooperative theological groups' on the British scene is represented in our opening section on 'Stories'. One particular area, however, from which the Church might justifiably expect some guidance on questions economic and political is that of Industrial Mission. There are several dozen full- and part-time chaplains to industry scattered throughout the country, in addition to countless thousands of laypeople. The chaplains form the Industrial Mission Association and recently their 'Theology Development Group' produced a short collection of essays.[12] It

begins with an article which attempts to meet the challenge industrial
mission in Britain is facing from the increasingly Marxist perspective
coming from Christians involved in industrial mission in Asia, Africa,
South America and also parts of Europe. It demonstrates some
defensiveness about the challenge of Third World 'Christian Marxists' but
does recognise that Marx may have something to say to British society.
Other essays argue for more analysis and for confining ourselves to what is
politically possible. Taken as a whole the collection exhibits an air of
confusion as to what theological political involvement could mean in the
economic industrial sphere. A somewhat gloomy final essay comments
that industrial mission in contemporary Britain seems more part of the
disease than the cure. It goes on to point to the basic defect in the analysis
expounded in Christian Social Tradition in Britain, that its dynamic is
moral rather than economic. The final call is for more analysis but the
impression left behind is that it may not be the kind of engaged and active
analysis which actually leads to real social change.

The Western country where political theology has most visibly surfaced
is the United States. There are perhaps advantages in politically-awakened
minority communities, the blacks, Hispanics, etc, and a proximity to the
source of much of the original thinking, the Latin American Church. In
1975, a large gathering took place in Detroit which attempted to relate
theological developments in both halves of the Continent. The resulting
volume, *Theology in the Americas*,[13] is a storehouse of information, ideas
and engagement which brings real encouragement to the aspiring commen-
tator on political theology in Britain. A five-year programme was set up to
relate theologically to various key dimensions of American society.

For the final section in this introductory survey we review briefly just
one author from North America, Joseph Petulla, a Catholic theologian
who has written *Christian Political Theology*,[14] a book which, it is claimed,
arises out of his experience in trying to organise young Christians in urban
areas to respond politically to the gospel imperative. Petulla draws deeply
on the writings and analyses of Marx, Engels and Lenin, and also more
contemporary socialists such as Mao and Castro. His intention is that
political theology should take up Marx's dictum for philosophy – its
purpose should be not merely to interpret the world but to change it.
'Political theology must be developed out of active praxis within the social
structures which are being described. An analysis of the alienating quality
of economic, political or social life must carry a personal bite or flavour
with it, the theologian must understand the personal measure of alienating
harm, or liberating change.' (p 5) In other words, the political theologian,
himself or herself, must be an actor and reflector within the situation or
process which is under analysis. There is no place for the disengaged
'objective' analytical stance – that incidentally may be the *real* message of

the Incarnation, which the 'Myth-debaters' entirely missed.

Petulla's central dialectic is between Alienation and Liberation, and his synthesis draws encouraging parallels between the Early Church, contemporary Christian Communities and the thoughts of Marx, Lenin and Mao. He develops the concept of 'onlook', which implies active involvement in the situation undergoing analysis. In his final section, on 'The Christian Dimensions', Petulla points out firstly – and crucially – that it is our pictures of God which lead us to either an active or passive relationship to society; secondly, he notes that evil and sin are not dealt with adequately by Marxism, and that Christianity's demand for 'permanent revolution' at both personal and social levels is vital; finally, he argues that the concept of 'celebration' is a central contribution by the Christian faith to a fully-developed human society.

One of Petulla's most helpful contributions is to expose once-for-all the fallacy and contradiction of the term 'Christian Marxist', which potentially devalues both philosophies (or faiths). He adopts the use of the adjective 'Marxian' to describe the use of Marxist method and analysis, without having to accept the whole of Marx's assumptions or conclusions. Thus the term 'Marxian Christian' is offered as a more accurate description of the Christian who appropriates Marxist principles in his or her economic and social analysis.

It would perhaps be incomplete to close this historical section of our Introduction without a reference to the BBC's Reith Lectures at the end of 1978, given by the historian Dr Edward Norman. His thesis was that Christianity was losing its eternal and supernatural dimension by becoming too closely identified with attempts to meet the practical needs of humanity and with the political and economic activities which ensue from such concerns. Suffice it to say that this whole book is an answer to that thesis, although we believe it is infinitely better answered by the prophets, both of the Old Testament and contemporary times, who have given comfort, liberty and even life to the cause of justice and peace in a Christian context, while Dr Norman (and many of us) have been sitting comfortably in our fireside chairs, 'thinking theology'.

Having undertaken a survey which seeks in an inevitably incomplete and selective way to write the prologue from which the first act of a British political theology might flow, it is time to describe the aims and methods of this volume. It has been done in a collective fashion, to demonstrate an important truth about the attempt to construct a political theology which will have a socialist perspective. This cannot be done fully or effectively by an individual, or even a small group. It is an enterprise which needs to be discussed and shared. In that sense the finished volume will only represent the first scene of a play which may need several decades for completion. It is hoped the readers will participate in the development of the drama, although as we point out a little later, those who are not involved in political action have little qualification for that participation. The debate is a dynamic one which rejects the static and 'objective' criticisms of many so-called theologians. Western Christianity has suffered already too much from their academic ennui.

Our method is firstly to take particular pieces of contemporary Christian action, which have political implications, and to tell them as illustrative stories or 'praxes' which describe possible forms of Christian engagement in society. They represent both the strengths and the weaknesses of what has developed, in Christian circles at least, out of the ferment of Western society in the late 1960s. They relate to what are hopefully the main areas of concern for a contemporary political theologian: racism, the women's movement, community living, the Church in the inner city and the battle against capitalism. The latter appears in two forms: the outlining of an alternative style of work – the co-operative; and the campaign against the Western financing of apartheid – ELTSA. If their weaknesses seem greater than their strengths, that may reflect both their incompleteness but also the reality of the Christian left in Britain today. They are, with a few others, all we have.

Secondly, we have tried to set our stories in an historical context, with three essays which give an insight into the development of Christian thinking on socialism, a stream of Christian thought and action which is stronger than might have been thought from the failure of the British Churches to respond to its challenges and insights. Tony Benn's article on the Levellers is a remarkable piece of writing from a politician who expresses pride in his own nonconformist Christian background and who, incidentally, embodies one of the very few real political options for socialist Christians as the 1980s begin. Ken Leech's historical review of the individuals and movements in the Christian socialist tradition since 1850 is a goldmine of information, and John Kent's post-Temple article brings us up to the beginning of the 1970s. The third section offers two perspectives on the situation of contemporary Britain, one from a Latin American theologian who has established a considerable reputation at world level while living, literally, in fear of his life in the maelstrom of political intrigue which is Argentina, and one from a Christian sociologist working at a British university.

Finally, under the heading 'Styles' (of Political Theology), we have gathered some more reflective articles, intended to give depth to our enterprise, without detracting from its immediacy, and offering different forms of theological interpretation for active political involvement by British Christians. These include Rex Ambler's exploration of how political theologies from other contexts may be drawn upon for the development of a political theology in Britain, the Christocentric radicalism of John

Vincent, grounded as it is in urban ministry and alternative forms of
theological education, and the complementary approaches of Pauline
Webb and Tom Cullinan to the question of whether and how the Church
may be an agent of social change in British society today. But perhaps the
most significant article, both because of the way it takes Marxism seriously
and because of its drawing out of the links between Christianity and
Marxism, is that of Fr Herbert McCabe. In a deceptively conversational
style, he offers an explosive analysis of the nature of capitalism, the class
struggle and the place of violence in the continuing conflict between
capital and labour. For McCabe there can be no defeat of the powerful and
self-seeking forces of capitalist society without violence. The combination
he outlines of Marxist thought and Christian practice exposes the real
demands that face the political theologian and the theologising politician
in a devastating manner.

The attempt is therefore to present various streams or dimensions of
Christian activity – the parish, the politico-theological campaign, the
external perspective, the academic reflection – together in the context of a
developing political theology. In our preparatory discussions, a comment
from a Christian activist expressed some doubt that this was possible,
particularly in the context of trying to relate academic university-based
theology to the efforts of those 'doing theology' in the inner city, the
protest movement, the factory and the AGM of the transnational
corporation. This points us to a question asked by Walter Hollenweger in
his foreword to Derek Winter's book on his South American journey.
Winter had decided against writing for an academic dissertation because it
would conflict with the needs of those for whom he wished to write. Does
this mean, asks Hollenweger, that 'we have not yet developed forms of
academic research which are both academically accurate and hopefully
relevant for the majority of people – those who support the university
with their taxes'? The answer to that question, with our present
educational and socio-political structure, is a resounding affirmative.

Ultimately, as Petulla pointed out in discussing the concept of 'God',
our understanding or picture of 'theology' informs our politics, the
corollary of which is that our politics strongly influences our theology.
Theology, 'theo-logos', is often translated 'god-talk', but that is not
enough. 'Logos' is more than words, or talk. The Logos of God was made
flesh in Jesus, rather more a dynamic than a static event. Theology has to
be done wherever Christians (and non-Christians) meet, in community
initiatives, political campaigns, trades union activities and 'action-for-
justice'. Only then will we see how the efforts of 'the professionals',
academics and clergy, to confine theological activity to the college or the
pulpit have deprived us (and them) of our spiritual birthright. Political
theology is not the only dimension of theology but it is arguably the most

important for society today. British churchmanship has lived for far too long on a false theological basis of privilege and superiority. It is time to let the Spirit, the Logos, of God break in again. The most effective place in which this happens is 'action-for-justice'. It is in the activity of seeking or creating justice in human society that the 'God' of theology most starkly and movingly appears. However, such action must take place within a stated theological context, rigid enough to give structure but sufficiently flexible to change as reflection follows action. Ultimately, the proponents and practitioners of political theology must be clear they are about nothing less than the transformation of human society and, under the direction of the Holy Spirit, the creating of the Kingdom of God.

References
1. John Hick (ed), *The Myth of God Incarnate*, SCM, 1977
2. Alistair Kee (ed), *A Reader in Political Theology*, SCM, 1974
3. Alistair Kee (ed), *The Scope of Political Theology*, SCM, 1978
4. Mervyn Stockwood, *The Cross and the Sickle*, Sheldon Press, 1978
5. Pauline Webb, *Salvation Today*, SCM, 1974
6. Ian Fraser, *The Fire Runs*, SCM, 1975
7. Derek Winter, *Hope in Captivity*, Epworth, 1978
8. Colin Winter, *Namibia*, Lutterworth, 1978
9. Cosmas Desmond, *Christians or Capitalists?*, Bowerdean Press, 1978
10. David Perman, *Change and the Churches*, Bodley Head, 1977
11. Trevor Beeson, *Britain Today and Tomorrow*, Collins, 1978
12. Industrial Mission Association, *Theology and Politics*, William Temple Foundation, 1978
13. Torres and Eagleson (eds), *Theology in the Americas*, Orbis, 1976
14. Joseph Petulla, *Christian Political Theology*, Orbis, 1972

ACTION

1. Urban Pilgrimage

David Moore

In 1977 the Bow Mission engaged Peter Chappell as a temporary youth worker, to look at the play needs of young people in the Bow area. Peter had just been released from prison as a result of his activity during the Free George Davis Campaign. We had hoped that during his five months with us he would be able to identify ways in which the Church could respond to the needs of young people. What happened — to everyone's surprise — was that a 5½-acre derelict site (which had been blocked up for over 10 years) became the focus of Peter's summer play project. Within a matter of weeks a small part of this site became opened up, turf was laid, a paddling pool was built and a small farm operated for the summer.

That summer scheme could not last, indeed it was not planned to last. But those hot summer weeks of 1977 saw the birth of a dream and an organisation. The dream was to turn the 5½-acre triangular site into a park which would be planned and worked on by local people. The organisation was the Bow Triangle Association and two years later it is a fully autonomous organisation, employing 14 people under a government employment scheme. When Peter Chappell began working for the Bow Mission in Holy Week 1977, a People's Park was the last thing we would have thought of. The wilderness is beginning to blossom.

The Bow Mission is a local organisation with its somewhat grubby fingers in a multitude of pies. It is always asking for money, it runs some fairly sophisticated projects, but it also has a record of muddle and incompetence. However, the Mission has come a long way from the paternalism and empire building of the past and aims to take the Gospel seriously in the context of East London.

Seeing what is
At the present time the Mission consists of four local churches, a students' hostel, an alcoholic project, a community work project, a youth centre

and sports ground, a race relations project including a literacy scheme, and a group which attempts to reflect theologically on what we are doing. Associated with the Mission are a foster home for 14 children, an organisation working with refugees and immigrants, a housing association, a community house which includes a toy library, the Namibia Peace Centre and a coordinating centre for single homeless projects in East London. All of these churches, projects and groups have seats on the Bow Mission Council (the Mission's governing body). The present members of the Council come from six different Christian denominations. Some members have no Christian affiliation at all. The jobs these people do also say something about the make-up of the Mission:

shop assistant	social workers	factory worker
play leader	foster mother	Church Army Captain
clerk	community worker	unemployed
teacher	building site foreman	a Namibian exile
packer	purchase clerk	printer
Ministers	housewife	immigrant welfare worker

The Mission, with its long history (founded in 1861) and previously traditional style, has in the last six years created a new constitution, opened up its decision-making mechanism to more and more people, and initiated several new projects.

Making space
Missions and settlements in East London have been notorious for the power invested in their leaders. This has been particularly true of Methodist Missions, where the Superintendent Ministers are invested with a wide range of constitutional powers and practical daily controls. The first major issue that had to be tackled six years ago was how truly to democratise the role of the ministry and that of the Mission's decision-making processes. To put it another way, how do you genuinely make space for others to participate? In attempting this we came to realise that many people seem to prefer the devil they know to the one they don't. There was considerable resistance to any move towards democratising the existing leadership.

Making space for others involves more than simply creating appropriate structures. It concerns the belief that God's Kingdom means including people who would normally be excluded from genuine participation. So an experimental constitution was created which enabled non-Methodists and indeed non-Christians to share in policy- and decision-making. This, together with the clipping of the Superintendent's wings, was a first step in the direction of that Kingdom.

Not knowing best

Making space for others (in my Father's house there's tons of room) is not only about inclusiveness. In order to pursue God's Kingdom we badly need to recognise our need of others. So the next major issue in the six-year period became that of trusting people. Or, to put it the other way round, not knowing best. It is difficult for Ministers or Priests not to believe, deep down, that they know best. It is easy to pay lip-service to the idea, but time and again mistaken or corrupted ideas of the relationship between ordination, authority, leadership and privilege by middle-class church workers in working class areas displays itself in actions and attitudes of superiority. This is particularly so in the assumptions about how you do certain things, eg running meetings, sharing information, making decisions, allocating resources.

This was clearly illustrated when we began a major redevelopment of our alcoholic project in 1976. This was much more than a simple reorganisation. We were attempting fundamentally to change our style and method of work. We were aiming at a way of working which would free us from our traditional paternalism and control. A style which would above all else, recognise and seek to develop the skills, abilities and resources of homeless alcoholics. In order to develop such a style and practical working methods, project workers had to trust the mission superintendent who was the symbol of paternalism and authority. On the other hand, the mission superintendent had to show the church leaders of pre-Mission Council days that the responsibility they had traditionally carried now belonged to project staff, none of whom were practising Christians. The people who were to operate the new programme used different language, symbols and methods in their work. It was a hard lesson to learn.

Sharing power

Making space for others and beginning to trust their judgments inevitably leads to facing the issue of power. This is not simply about who wins the vote on a particular issue but rather about the basic models on which we work — models which are often deeply submerged beneath the public face of our life as a church or as individuals. All institutions have ways of maintaining power — some subtle, some crude. The Church is no exception. Until our new constitution was formed the basic control was financial. The Mission had 19 different bank accounts and it was almost impossible in the course of a hurried business meeting for anyone, except the two or three key figures, to unravel what became known by one member of staff as the 'money mystery'. Sharing power means sharing information and decision-making. It also means working in such a way that you maximise the number of people participating, from the creating of budgets or plans to spending the money or doing the work. We have made some headway in sharing power by the way we present our accounts and make our decisions.

In spite of all its problems, the Church in the inner city can be in an enormously privileged position. Its full-time leaders often have the potential to wield considerable power. The question is: how do we see and use such power? Do we speculate with good deeds and so accumulate more power in order that we might do more good? Do we attempt to be a positive 'force' for good, so that the more power we have, the more effective we can be?

If we believe God's Kingdom is a present reality as well as a future hope, it seems obvious that 'means are as important as ends'. The present is always the important time for Christians (the Day of Salvation), for it is in the present that we have to live our testimony to the existence of the Kingdom.

Over all the questions of power lies the shadow of the Cross, the symbol of powerlessness. If powerlessness is the way into the Kingdom, then we have to get rid of the power we have! We do this, not by abandoning our responsibilities but by sharing that power in order that those who are powerless may begin to have some edge on us. How else can the last become first?

Not surprisingly, we haven't got very far with this!

Seeing through dark glass clearly
East London is the kind of place where it is almost impossible not to be impressed by something of magnitude every day — good things, corrupt things, beauty, pollution, cultural diversity, injustice, spontaneity, racism, alcoholism, earthy vitality, homelessness, bustling street market, bureaucracy. Seeing clearly what is really happening is very difficult. Seeing issues clearly inevitably means making enemies or at least creating misunderstandings.

Three years ago a Minister of the Mission became involved in the 'Free George Davis' Campaign. Because of that involvement he was on the receiving end of considerable criticism and abuse. Few people seemed to understand his reasons for involvement in such a controversial issue. Alongside the personal question of a man's wrongful imprisonment was an issue of equal importance. When a group of people have exhausted every acceptable legal, constitutional and lobbying tactic in order to get their voice heard on such a burning issue as 20 years' wrongful imprisonment, what does the Church do when nobody in a position of influence appears to listen? When those who have power, law and media control at their disposal simply ignore the voices that are raised, must not the Church stand with those who cry for justice? Taking sides in the George Davis Campaign inevitably meant being associated with digging up Test wickets and the outrage that followed. Many people argued the rights and wrongs of the Test wicket issue. Many argued the question of innocence or guilt. Few detractors were prepared to consider how, in our society, the voice of an unpopular, dispossessed group could be heard. Fewer still dared consider the question of controlling the media from the bottom by 'making front page news'. Seeing the real issues is always hard. Much of the time we fail to do so. When we do it is always disturbing and uncomfortable. If the Church is serious in its quest to carry Christ's cross it must expect such discomfort.

Sticking it out

The six years we have been 'at it' at Bow have passed remarkably quickly. There are always temptations to take short cuts, to change direction or simply to squabble amongst ourselves.

We believe that the work we are engaged in will only be complete when local church members and associated groups really begin to call the tune. The Mission will be where it should be when, say, a staff member leaves and the Council starts to ask, 'Do we really need to replace him or her or can we do this work ourselves?' Then we will know that the Spirit has begun to seize power.

2. The Christian Parity Group

Una Kroll

The Christian Parity Group is a network of Christians who are committed to pray and work for the full partnership of women and men everywhere.

The Group was born in 1972, out of love and anger. At that time the government of the day published a Green Paper which suggested that the 'cash in hand' Family Allowances, which had always been paid directly to mothers through the Post Office, should be taken away from them and given to the fathers instead. This proposal caused widespread dismay. It was felt that if the government proposals were carried out many children would never benefit from the money that was originally intended for them.

Many women decided to petition Parliament to stop the plans. A protest march was planned. Some of us who were Christians decided to contact some 20 well known, well established church women's organisations to invite their support. We were told that none of them would be going. A variety of excuses were given, most of which implied that respectable church women ought not to ally themselves with the kind of disreputable people who belonged to the Women's Liberation Movement. It was then that love and anger collided and we decided to join the march and to learn more about the Women's Movement.

We discovered that the institutional Churches had virtually no contacts with the secular women's movement. Very few church people had any detailed knowledge of the ways in which sexism ruins the relationships between women and men. Sexism is a coined word which has affinities with racism. It describes any 'attitude, action or institutional structure which systematically subordinates a person or group on grounds of sex'.

That first march, our subsequent studies and our involvement in the secular fight against sexism alerted us to the rightness of Christian participation in the struggles of oppressed people to be liberated from the slavery of sexism. We began with women, but quickly discovered that men could be as oppressed as women by this evil and so we have included men in the Group from the beginning. We are also linked with the struggle for the human rights of homosexuals, bisexuals and transsexuals.

Like all liberation theologies ours is an inductive theology which springs from our own and other people's experiences of oppression. Reflection on the Bible and on the history of the early Church supports our belief that 'for freedom Christ has set us free' (*Gal* 5:1) and that we 'are all one in Christ Jesus' (*Gal* 3:28). Our objective, therefore, is to claim that freedom which Christ won for all people. We aim to make a specifically Christian contribution to the struggle of women and men to discover the kind of relationships that will lead them to the freedom of mutuality and co-responsibility. We, therefore, actively support any movement or activity which is going on in the community to alter the attitudes and structures of society which oppress men and women and prevent them from discovering each other's humanity.

Our work is rooted in prayer and theological reflection. We believe that true contemplation of God will find its expression in action so we are unashamedly activist, and we deliberately invite our members to make a personal commitment to action in the areas of the struggle in which they are most interested and concerned. Every member is free to act according to conscience.

So far members of the Group have lobbied to secure the payment of Family Allowances to mothers. Some of us joined with others to secure the passage of the Sex Discrimination Bill (1975). We have continued to press for the reform of tax laws and social security systems where they discriminate against individuals or sections of the community. Some of us are active in the Women's Movement. Some concentrate on the rights of homosexuals and transsexuals.

Since the Church itself is oppressed by sexism many members of the Group are trying to alter the oppressively male symbolism of the language, customs and structures which prevent the Churches from reflecting the nature of God to the people of God. God's image needs to be liberated from the anthropomorphic fantasies which have accumulated around the Trinity. The people of God need to be liberated from the masculine language, rituals and male-only ministries which oppress them and prevent women and men from discovering their true partnership in Christ. Those of us engaged in this work know that revolutionary changes will be needed in the ordained ministries if they are to serve the future generations to the best of their ability. We have, therefore, concentrated our attention on the symbolism of priesthood and urged all Churches to admit women to full partnership with men in the ordained ministries. We have made two television programmes (1973 and 1977) about the ordination of women and have sponsored a tour of England by the first nun-priest to be ordained in the United States of America: Canon Mary Simpson came here in 1978.

Since November 1978, when the Church of England voted against allowing women to be ordained as deacons, priests and bishops, we have helped to start the Movement for the Ordination of Women, whose single-minded aim is to promote the Ordination of Women in the Anglican Churches of the British Isles. As individual women are likely to be disbarred from Holy Orders for at least a decade, we are raising financial support for some of the women who have decided to emigrate in order to follow God's call.

We intend to continue to take part in theological dialogue and in symbolic protest and constructive criticism of all these policies which oppress women and men in the Church. We have participated in the setting up of the Christian Women's Information and Research Service to raise money for women in all the Churches and to coordinate the efforts of many small groups like our own who are working for the abolition of sexist oppression in all the Churches.

The Group is not an organisation but a network of people. We have no regular income, committees or special leaders at present. We operate on individual initiative and consensus. Since it is deliberately small, poor and activist in emphasis, the Group will continue to exist only so long as it is necessary for its members to participate in its projects. Obsolescence is guaranteed by the work of Christ. Redundancy will be a pleasure.

3. CARAF

Basil Manning

Britain is a multiracial society but Britain is also a racist society, a society in which the Prime Minister can whip up latent racism by talking about black people as undesirable elements of whom white people have 'natural' fears of being swamped. Black people are clearly seen as 'the problem' and there is a lack of recognition that the phenomenon of white racism permeates the whole of society, not only the fascist National Front. *White racism* has yet to be recognised as one of the largest social and psychological problems this country has to face.

Christians bear a great deal of the responsibility for colluding with this failure to face the issue of racism. There is a charitable approach to the Gospel, leading to a distortion which causes the victims of a social evil actually to be regarded as the evil itself. So the poor are seen as the problem, rather than the rich whose economic policies create poverty.

Ask the average person in the pew about Jesus' teaching on poverty and wealth, and the texts which would be uppermost in their minds would be those of the Final Judgement in *Matthew* 25 and the story of the rich young ruler in *Matthew* 19. In the interpretation of the *Matthew* 25 we are led to believe that those who fed the hungry, gave water to the thirsty and visited those sick and in prison will be destined for eternal blessing, and those who did not for eternal damnation. This thinking is strengthened by the interpretation of Jesus' message to the young ruler to sell all and give it to the poor. It's the 'giving to the poor' which western Christianity has highlighted in this text. But Jesus at this point is not concerned with the poor but rather with how this man's wealth affected his capacity to act in human rather than in economic terms. Empty yourself of your wealth is the message, so that you can relate to others on equal terms again. This is not the overriding interpretation placed on the passage by British Christians today.

Western Christianity, bold in its accusation that Christianity in the

Third World is too willing to syncretise with other cultural norms, has been less critical of its own syncretism with white-dominated capitalism. It now has locked within its bowels the preservation of the status quo: it needs both the rich and the poor to make it work, in order that the poor may continue to receive from the bounty of the rich. This thinking has unfortunately influenced Christian thinking on racism and fascism. We are exhorted to 'do something' about the problem, to be 'positive and constructive', rather than 'negative', to circumvent the effects of racism to build a 'harmonious society'. We are told it is not helpful to be 'against things'. So the advent of Christians Against Racism and Fascism (CARAF) in the latter part of 1977 was greeted with a great deal of resistance. People's desire to preserve the status quo conflicted with their wish to be seen to be doing something positive about 'the problem'. So, we are pleased to spend human and financial resources to pick up the pieces from the effects of racism, without making a concerted attack on white racism in its individual or institutional forms.

It was with these concerns in mind that a number of Christians met at the initiative of the Student Christian Movement at Wick Court near Bristol in June 1977. The greatest concern at this consultation was the lack of Christian commitment to an unequivocal opposition to racism and fascism and the growth of fascist groups in Britain. We noted the 'positive work' being done by the British Council of Churches' Community and Race Relations Unit in making British Churches aware of the effects of racism, and in giving grants to self-help groups struggling on limited resources to counter the disadvantages which blacks inherit from institutionalised racism. Little, however, was being done by the churches vigorously to oppose racism, be it in the National Front, or in the utterances of some ecclesiastical leaders, or in Society's structures which perpetuate exploitation and discrimination.

It was clear to those at the Wick meeting that the National Front were both exploiting the racism in British society and using a racist platform for fascist political ends. After repatriation they would turn to the control of other groups – the unions, the Churches, students, and other minorities in Britain. More importantly, the almost absurd policies which they were allowed to hawk on the streets while masquerading as a legitimate political party were setting the tone for equally frightening measures being proposed by the major political parties as a 'fall-back' position. These now include tighter controls to delay the reunion of families from the Asian subcontinent; the entrenchment of 'patriality' in the nationality laws; a system of internal control for 'immigrants'; the setting up of the Illegal Immigrant Intelligence Unit; and the extension of racism into the enforcement of law through the disproportionate use of 'sus' (Section 4 of the Vagrancy Act 1824) and 'conspiracy' charges against black people.

Clearly the climate created by the National Front was pushing ordinary Christians into acquiescence with proposed measures which seemed less threatening by comparison.

A bold initiative was needed to expose these measures and our collusion with them. The National Front, which was setting the tone for such extreme changes, equally needed to be exposed and discredited. With massive support from 250 representatives of all shades of theological persuasion, CARAF was launched in January 1978.

The success of that inaugural meeting was tempered by behind-the-scenes efforts to emasculate the initiative even before it got off the ground. There was a great debate about whether the British Council of Churches should circulate the invitations to its membership. The church centre in which the meeting was to be held suddenly became unavailable through an 'administrative error'. However, lack of enthusiasm changed to a positive commitment to the initiative once it became clear that the response to the Inaugural Conference was overwhelming. CARAF, from its inception, had no illusions about the difficulties it would face. Some Christians already had reservations about 'fascism' in the title. The sterile argument about the need to be not *against* but *for* something reared its ugly head and continues to be a problem for some.

Herein lies the fundamental dilemma for CARAF: will it continue to oppose racism and fascism from a Christian perspective, or fall into the trap of caring for 'the victims'? Is CARAF to attack white racism, or continue to campaign about the effects while never addressing itself to the cause? At first CARAF carefully balanced its approach. The first executive committee of CARAF made great efforts to fulfil the desire of the Inaugural Assembly that it should not be a top heavy organisation but should recognise that work at the grass roots was imperative. Regional contacts were identified and local groups were encouraged to develop their own styles of work related to the issues in their area. This has largely involved educating the white community and initiating solidarity work in the churches on campaign issues already articulated in the black community, such as the 'sus' campaign and Immigration and Nationality Laws. But CARAF was also to be a movement which would enthuse Christians sufficiently that they would feel compelled by their faith to take to the streets when necessary to demonstrate their total abhorrence of racist and fascist ideology.

In April 1978 CARAF set out to test the extent of this Christian commitment by planning a Silent March of Christian Witness through London. It was hoped that Christians in their thousands would come out to bear witness on that day. Despite a ban on all marches imposed by the Home Secretary, CARAF proceeded with arrangements for a National Act of Christian Witness in Hyde Park. Just over a thousand Christians vicariously participated in the symbolic cleansing of the Union Jack — the symbol of the nation, so soiled by exploitation, colonisation and racism. As we participated in that act of penitence we knew that we were doing it for the majority of Christians in the Church as well. For all alike had been affected by the myths, propaganda and lies which flow from a history of colonialism and oppression and which now permeate the consciousness of individuals and the social, political and economic structures of the nation.

At the Hyde Park Rally CARAF supporters tried to celebrate the richness of our multiracial society. But it was not easy, for the need to come to a new understanding of the gospel message of *rebirth* and to relate this to our legacy of racism was clearly spelt out. The essence of such rebirth is that through repentance we turn around in our tracks on this issue of racism and go the opposite way. Only when white Christians have undergone that *metanoia* will they be able genuinely to meet black Christians and work and worship together. For the present we all experience but a shadow of that 'shalom'.

How will we do it? Can CARAF engender that repentance when the argument is still about whether the phenomenon of white racism is a reality or not? Does confronting the National Front cause us to see so clear an image of ourselves and our nation that we dare not look into the mirror? If we cannot recognise that the *real problem* is white racism and the institutions which breed on the racist and classist nature of British society, the futile argument about the wisdom of being 'against' something will continue. The limited resources of CARAF must be used not to engage in this sterile debate but to confront the principalities and powers of racism and fascism in Britain today, and to challenge all British Christians to do the same.

4. Co-operatives in Northern Ireland

Des Wilson

Across the Northern part of Ireland, from Donegal to Antrim, citizens'
co-operatives have grown up during the past 30 years. They were a
response to local problems of unemployment and emigration; in many
cases they were created by Catholic clergy. They were also in places a
response to the failure of government to relieve social problems.

At first, because of their origin and aims, the philosophy underlying
these co-operatives was limited – it is better to have work than not to
have it. But soon there was added the idea that people should take a hand
in their own fate, that if industry had to be built from the ground up then
all those who did the work on the ground should make the required
decisions.

This was often looked upon as a radical doctrine and some very
conservative people, including clergy, were branded 'communist' when
what they were trying to do was extend the areas in which people could
make decisions of consequence.

The growth of co-operatives in Ireland over a long period has been a
response of local people to urban and rural need; it brought many such
anomalies and did not produce a coherent philosophy. It was given a fresh
dimension in Northern Ireland in the troubled period of 1968-69.

In 1968-69 there was an upsurge of feeling about the right of citizens
to take part in government. There was no correspondingly strong demand
for participation in industry; the demand that workers should sit on
management boards would not have brought a single worker out on to the
streets. The co-operative ideal had been long in existence and, since it
included the ideal of workers creating enterprises, managing them and
sharing profits according to their own needs rather than the desires of
shareholders, it took on a new look in many people's minds from 1968-69
onwards. Co-operatives expressed the citizens' desire to have a say in their
own affairs, including industry; other movements were concerned with

government, education, Church affairs, etc. That is, the co-operative movement was now part of a wider movement and was more significant than for many years in the past. Those who founded co-operatives in Northern Ireland from 1970 onwards had this very much in mind.

At this time also the co-operative ideals appealed to Protestants in Northern Ireland, who were now beginning to have serious doubts about the goodwill and the ability of government to solve their problems. Community enterprise also appealed to some citizens who wished for an alternative to military action for political change. Since this wish existed among some of those who had previously been in military organisations, there was a danger that the government would use the co-operative movement in order to defeat the military campaigns of some of the armed citizens' organisations, thus bringing the movement into counter-revolutionary politics, with damaging results for the movement.

Meanwhile, interest in the possibilities of co-operatives had awakened in some people who were capable both of working out a philosophy of action and techniques of survival and development which had seemed impractical in the past, eg co-operative banks, government support on the co-operatives' terms, etc.

Many of those who founded and supported co-operatives in Ireland were Christian, some of them clergy. But the movement never received notable support from the churches as such. Indeed at times the co-operatives were overshadowed by the suggestion that within them there must be dangerous latent tendencies. Once popular decision-making upset the traditional framework within which Christian teaching about industrial relations had been created, there would have to be some unwelcome rethinking of relationships in other areas of life as well. After all, if the demarcation lines between management and workers in industry were to be so blurred then perhaps the lines between ruler and ruled, between hierarchy and people, would be blurred as well. The Church's ideal of 'an honest day's work for an honest day's pay' had never been updated to accommodate co-operative sharing, or elective industrial management. Those who helped form the co-operatives had to make up their own philosophy — and theology — as they went along, beginning with the concept of the ability of every person to create, the right of every person to work and live in an area of choice, the obligation of everyone to create a society in which initiative would always be welcome but would not be allowed to lead to selfishness.

The inability of the Christian Churches to develop a philosophy, or theology, of co-operatives was surprising since co-operatives seemed to express in work-a-day terms what the Churches were preaching on Sundays.

Co-operatives in country areas in Ireland had a better chance of survival than those in the cities. The country areas, however poor, had some natural resources and their clergy who were willing to do it had the time needed for the business of founding co-operatives. The city was very different, with clergy overloaded with chores and citizens who often lacked a feeling of identity, all of them suffering from lack of obvious natural resources. In the country areas co-operatives were often founded upon markets and agricultural business; in the city this central, living activity was lacking. Gradually, however, it became clear that co-operatives in the city which were concerned with buying and selling foodstuffs were likely to be more quickly successful than those which tried to manufacture goods. In both city and country the co-operatives, being something which arose from the needs and the genius of local people, were likely to begin from what the people were good at already. Thus there were attempts to create co-operatives in urban areas based on food distribution, crafts and knitted goods. It was an attractive prospect for people feeling their way, but the ideal sometimes suffered a rude shock when confronting the realities of the modern industrial world.

A knitwear co-operative in the Ballymurphy area of Belfast, for example, began in 1970, employing 16 people, all of whom received wages equal to or above the current rates. It built a new factory. Knitwear is a competitive industry with profit margins at times as low as two to three per cent. The co-operative went out of business in 1978 because it had not the markets and cash flow necessary to survive. Another co-operative in the same area created an industrial estate and a building group. The wages were on a par with current rates but there was no surplus for distribution. The building trade and promotion of industry are difficult and once again the lesson was learned that while local skills may be excellent, management skills of a high order are also needed, and these are often difficult to attract into an underdeveloped area. A blockmounting co-operative in the same area employs four people, pays current wage rates and has some funds for further distribution. It is very successful and will probably have to diversify its products — perhaps needing some help from outside its own area.

Here is a rich field for the philosophers and theologians if they are willing to explore it; what is in question is the discovery of the value of what people can do when they act in response to needs which they see and feel, and when they begin to realise their immense ability to use their talents to fulfil these needs. Unfortunately, so much of our thinking about work has been rooted in concepts of the industrial revolution that it is difficult to extricate it now that the industrial revolution has been spun out and a new phase of mankind's understanding of work is ready to emerge.

When the co-operatives came into contact with the world of organised business, some of them foundered. Some succeeded, but all of them learned lessons. The difficulty of producing locally-made goods at 'economic' prices was one of them. No one could afford to buy, or sell, for its real value in money terms, much of the kind of work which, for example, a woman may knit or crochet for her friends and relatives, unless there is a very well-developed luxury market available. To turn her work into something commercially viable would be to enter the highly expensive, and fickle, world of fashion and luxury goods, which requires adaptability of a high order. When the fashions change, the workers will have to become skilled at producing something else, and that kind of adaptability may not come unless with government help. That is, there is seldom now, as far as one can see, such a thing as a pure self-help scheme. Sooner or later most schemes become local enterprises with government backing. A new problem of independence and initiative now arises and perhaps a new definition of independence, or of government authority, is needed.

Should a Christian be particularly interested in industrial and other kinds of co-operatives? Is there anything specially Christian about them?

One could answer that question by saying that co-operatives are one means of rescuing work from the unchristian usages and attitudes which have bedevilled it in the factory age. The trouble was not only that people had to work in cramped or unhealthy conditions. It was very much that in this system, as in others which preceded it, the human being was an instrument to be taken up and laid aside when the comfort of the master required it. To an astonishing degree the Church not only connived at but even created such conditions of servitude. And it was not eventually the outgoing generosity of Christians which brought about changes in conditions of work but rather a slow, agonised struggle to enact suitable laws, every one of which was contested every inch of the way. Paul, writing about how some people in his day celebrated the Eucharist, pointed out how shamefully the rich enjoyed their riches while the poor looked hungrily on. The Eucharist was not only a celebration of what ought to be but also an awful symbol of what actually was. And the two were horrifyingly different. For the Christian the co-operatives could be extensions into industry of the sharing which is celebrated in his Eucharist. Unless this style of sharing *is* extended into industry, the Eucharist makes as little sense now among industrialists as it did among Paul's selfish Corinthians.

So the fundamental ideals of Christianity are important in this industrial context: that is, the sharing of God's creation, the joint participation by all in making decisions, and the common privilege of renewing the face of the earth. Christian theology should have something exciting and fresh to say about this. But it should have something penitential as well as exciting and fresh to say about what human dignity and work really mean. Perhaps the co-operative ideal can help us to restate our theology.

We have become used to the idea that working in factories — being 'employed' — gives a person his or her dignity. People may be 'employed' in many ways, but let us think in terms of factories. To say that a man with certain skills, or with few skills, cannot be allowed his human dignity unless he is 'employed' gives factories a significance and power which they do not possess; yet it is said over and over again by Christians who seem to mistake the philosophies of industrial development for Christian theology. Christians believe that people have dignity because they were created by God the Father, renewed by the Son and are filled with the Holy Spirit. To say or imply, as many Christians do, that people do not possess human dignity unless they are 'gainfully employed' in industry or organised services, comes near to blasphemy.

Work then should be of such a kind that it expresses this superb dignity which Christians believe men, women and children have. Those who admire the co-operative ideal would say, with some justification, that work in a system which involves as much decision-making as possible by all is the only kind that can express human dignity adequately, because human beings are first and foremost creatures who can make choices and decisions and who have been given responsibility for their decisions by God Himself. If God gives such responsibility, we should be content to see it given and shared in every area of life, including industry.

This seems an irrefutable argument which in modern industrial conditions makes more and more sense. As always, good theology has something to say to good business, understanding business as the organisation of work by and for those who actually do it.

5. Ashram Community House

Roy Crowder

The call to form communities of economic sharing is obviously at the heart of the gospel. Jesus and his disciples, as well as the Jerusalem Church in *Acts* 2, held their goods in common. Equally obviously there is a contradiction between such communities of economic sharing and the shape of British society today, based as it is on huge inequalities of wealth and income. But the very contradictory nature of the communitarian movement in contemporary society means it must be established in a hardheaded, realistic way, because it is liable to challenge every value incarnate in society's structure and practice.

Things in common

In the summer of 1976 the members of our Ashram Community House in inner-city Sheffield began to discuss what it would mean to share all our incomes in common. The House was established five years before and members had shared a proportion of their incomes since then. By 1976 the membership of the community house had changed and become more committed over a longer term. We were used to sharing many aspects of our lives and possessions and felt the pressure to go further. The pressure came from our intention to live as a community and discussions about what that meant; it came from the gospel record of Jesus-centred communities; also from job-changes within our own lives; and from the need to practise in a small way the ideals we held for society.

Now, two and a half years later, it is hard to evaluate what has happened. It feels to have been a profound alteration, putting our community living and relationships onto a different plane from before. First, it has been an overwhelmingly positive change, despite the fears for us expressed by some friends and relatives. We have had no major upsets or squabbles, or broken relationships over what to do with our money. Our major challenge has been devising an accounting system to control the flow of money. On the way we have realised how inhospitable our society is to people sharing money and supporting each other. Banks, building societies, insurance companies, tax authorities and local authorities, etc, have no legal category with which to recognise a community's existence and relate to it. Only the nuclear family (however short its duration or minimal its sharing) is recognised as a corporate way of living by these institutions. For instance, our local planning authority tried to close us down through the manipulation of discretionary fire regulations because they would not accept that we were a single household.

Our income sharing has resulted in many things. Mainly it has given us more power over more resources. We have more money to give away, though not perhaps as much as we hoped when we started planning. We are also able to make loans out of our combined cash flow to support local alternative work projects. Our sharing has increased and expressed our reliance upon one another. Those of us earning low incomes are supported by the income of the others to do the work we think is most important, rather than most lucrative. So we are led to ask basic questions about the value of jobs.

In another way our corporate control over a quite large total income (however modestly it averages out) makes us more powerful than our neighbours and gives us greater security than many have, distancing us from some of the local common concern. For instance, we can more easily benefit from the lower costs of bulk purchase, and delays in wage payment which bring real hardship to others are easily cushioned in our household budget. To that extent we need constantly to re-examine, as a community focused on the Jesus story in an area of need, our commitment to belong to our neighbourhood.

Life in common
Ashram Community House in Pitsmoor, an inner-city area on the north-east side of Sheffield, was opened in 1971. Today, six of us, two women and four men, in our twenties and thirties, support our community in a variety of jobs. There are two lecturers and a teacher, a cook and trade union official, an advice centre organiser and a computer programmer. We have been concerned both to develop the internal life of the community and to engage as residents in the concerns, issues and celebrations of the diverse and fascinating area in which we live.

The internal life of the community has always involved shared domestic work, especially cooking; shared finance; shared decision-making, without a 'leader' but with leadership emerging from particular people for particular things; shared worship, mainly at our weekly eucharist; shared jokes, drinking and dancing; shared elations and upsets.

The community has also always shared in the life of the neighbourhood.

Our property is available. Free legal information was dispensed from our surgery for years and all sorts of local meetings use one of our front rooms. Our work is often local. Ashram members have held jobs as a playbus leader/driver, a home-school liaison teacher who lives in her school's catchment area, and a housing rights adviser at the local Citizens' Advice Bureau. Our life as a Christian congregation is related to neighbouring churches. As members of the Sheffield Inner City Ecumenical Mission we are related to seven other traditional and 'alternative' churches. Our social life is also found in the neighbourhood. Groups of children and young people latch on to us from time to time, especially near to 5 November. Some of them we have known now since early childhood. We have networks of friends, especially among the West Indian population, in particular pubs, working men's clubs and congregations. Most of our political actions have also sprung from our local inner city area where low pay and heavy unemployment, demolition and redevelopment, the run-down and withdrawal of facilities, bedevil and limit people's lives. So we have engaged in action groups over many issues: the closure of swimming baths and schools; the demolition or improvement of houses; the planning of estates and roads; the provision of playschemes and youth clubs; the negative and debilitating way in which authorities define and survey our neighbourhood.

Action in common
One of our most significant and long-term commitments has been with a group of other residents in the local neighbourhood action group. A few months after we had moved in and become part of the area, we helped call together a public meeting to discuss the proposed demolition of our area's substantial houses. The council's plan had not been discussed with any local people when it designated us as a clearance area. We thought it was right to work with people to build up an indigenous organisation which could speak and fight on behalf of the residents' wishes. After more than three years' hard work of meetings, surveys, arguments, neighbourliness, interviews, letters, depression, lobbying, typing, laughs and celebrations, we were declared a Housing Action Area. Thus improvements were to be made to the housing stock and the environment. There followed nearly five years more of meetings, etc, as the detailed improvement work was carried out and checked over. It is not over yet.

It is not easy to assess the impact of all this. A few houses still need basic repair and amenities. Areas of cleared land, where houses had to be demolished, mar the environment. But there has been a definite and overall improvement. The housing standard is higher. Though often too late, the debilitating effect of planning blight has at long last been lifted. Above all, people have experienced the possibility of determining some

improvement in their lives rather than being overwhelmed by an
environment deteriorating beyond their control.

Too many people have suffered too deeply the decline and collapse of
their houses, both in value and fabric, to speak of 'improvement' glibly.
Nonetheless, things have changed for the better. Too many people have
been humiliated by the lack of respect, faith and knowledge accorded to
them by council members and officers to talk glibly of 'participation'.
But a decision to demolish has been reversed. Most important of all, there
has been detailed joint oversight of the improvement programme.

Gospel and politics in common
How does this relate to the life, to the career, if we like, of Jesus the
Nazarene? The actions so far described, with the exception of Christian
worship, might be dismissed, and sometimes are, because they are like the
actions of other groups in similar places who 'do social work' with no
reference to Jesus.

The gospel, however, does not make such an easy distinction between
the ministry, death and resurrection of Jesus and the society of men,
women and children. The 'Way' Jesus pointed to happened in and through
the social relations of people. Where else could it happen?

So our lifestyle and political actions struggle to be a sign or expression
of that reality or way of living to which Jesus pointed. What we are
involved in is not then 'social work' as such or anything like it. Nor is it
just personal or political action either.

The movement of Jesus and his disciples was part of a spectrum of
renewal groups within Jewish society struggling to discover and express
what God's Rule — the Kingdom of Heaven — would be like. So the
common struggle of Pharisees, Essenes, Zealots and other renewal groups
was basically affirmed by Jesus. But their answers were all challenged. The
interest groups within society clearly staked out the political options
which everyone had to choose between. Jesus refused to take the choice
but did not claim to be neutral, spiritual or misunderstood. The Herodian
collaboration with a Gentile power; the Sadducean 'social responsibility'
religion of not rocking the boat; the Pharisaic reassertion of a
legalistically defined system for controlling all behaviour, including the
political; the Essene disciplined withdrawal from practical politics 'until
the conflagration come!'; and the Zealot mirror-image — violent opposition
to the Roman Rule — were none of them the way to Jesus. His establishment
of 'the Twelve' as an alternative Israel was a provocative, parabolic sign of
God's Way. It did not face political annihilation on the Cross because
people misunderstood it, or because it only had 'spiritual' significance,
but precisely because His Way posed such a fundamental threat to the
power base of the Pharisees, Sadducees and Romans alike.

Spirit in common

For us, then, the way of Jesus, that is to say the happenings of his ministry, with a group of disciples, in a particular society, at a particular time, can be a model or measure for us in our time. It encourages us to explore alternative ways of organising the patterns of work, reward and decision-making within a small community. This is a distinct, practical achievement, it is a better way of living together, we find, and it is a sign to others. It encourages us to join with anyone we can to act for justice, increased awareness and participation in the neighbourhood. This is an achievement of better living conditions, it is an answer to what people are asking for and not what is thought good for them, and also it is a sign to the wider world of how change can occur.

Our worship is whatever keeps our mind focused on the figure of Jesus in his world and its overlay on our world. For us it mainly takes the form of a eucharist or shared meal where people's concerns and celebrations are voiced and a Bible passage read.

Our spirituality is whatever gives us access to the spirit that was in Jesus. For us it mainly means just living with and joining in the good times and bad times of those who share our neighbourhood. Many of them are the despised, the patronised, the exploited in British society. They are those driven into, or trapped in, our ghettos and asylums. But there, in the places the Church has shunned over the years to avoid contamination, the spirit of Jesus is recognised most readily.

6. The ELTSA Story

David Haslam

The situation in South Africa throws into sharp contrast the difference between 'reformist' and 'radical' political theology. Many Christians will reluctantly accept that political considerations must enter into the practice of Christianity when factors such as that of racism come into play. They will agree that, although opposition to racism is not the Church's prime task, it should indeed take some action when racism has become as entrenched as it has in Southern Africa. However, the response of these Christians and of the institutional Church is basically to see such action as additional, even peripheral, to its main task, which is 'Mission'. To the radical 'political Christian', to fight against racism is in itself mission. The experience of the 'End Loans to Southern Africa' (ELTSA) group, formed to oppose all bank lending to South Africa, bears out this analysis of the differing views on political theology.

History
Banks based in Europe and later in North America have always played an important role in the subjugation and exploitation of the African people. It is important to set in an historical context the role they now play. From the first discoveries of rich agricultural land, of an abundance of mineral ores, and of gold itself, banks became involved in the commerce of the developing colonialist structures. They financed the expansion of farming, mining and later manufacturing, and of course they profited greatly from South Africa's abundant resources and its cheap labour.

Gradually, however, African resistance manifested itself during the 1950s and 1960s, and the more informed and militant of the black people took up a position which demanded the withdrawal of all Western interests and involvement in South Africa. The banks, along with the enterprises they financed, came under attack and, for the first time, sympathisers in the West began to understand, firstly, what had been really happening in Southern Africa and, secondly, what could be done about it. In the late 1960s, opposition was mobilised in the American Churches to 'revolving loans' being made by United States banks to companies operating in South Africa and, from an initial position that they were not of course in any way supporting apartheid by their 'neutral involvement', the banks eventually withdrew the loans. This claim of 'apolitical neutrality' appears time and again in the debate on the morality of investment in Southern Africa, the clear fact that by lending money to somebody who is involved in an immoral business one is then participating in that business appears always to have escaped the bankers of the 'Christian' West. Yet by their involvement they have enabled the apartheid regime to become as financially sound, militarily impregnable and economically self-sufficient as it is now.

The Campaign

In 1973, from a source high up in an international bank, a Church group in the United States received documents showing that a number of European banks, united together in the European-American Banking Corporation (EABC), based in New York, was making loans direct to the South African government. The ensuing campaign involved pressure groups in the Netherlands, the United Kingdom and the United States of America and also the World Council of Churches. It further revealed to what extent banks in Europe, North America and even Japan were involved in financing apartheid.

In Britain ELTSA (End Loans to Southern Africa) was formed directly to try to stop the EABC loans, in which Midland Bank was participating. During 1974 and 1975, a number of Church bodies, some of whom were shareholders in the bank, were approached and they in turn approached the bank. The response was negative, Midland taking the position that bankers could not decide on the morality of the purposes for which they lent and avoiding answering such questions as whether they would have lent to Nazi Germany in the 1930s. In 1976 ELTSA therefore organised the first-ever Resolution to a British company on a social or moral issue. This in itself was a lesson in the anti-democratic nature of the financial world, as one hundred shareholders, holding over 10,000 shares between them, had to be found to support such a Resolution. The Central Finance Board of the Methodist Church agreed to take the role of leading sponsor of the Resolution and support was also obtained from a number of other Church shareholders, including the Church Commissioners, as well as universities, local authorities and charities. Many colleges and even Church bodies, however, declined to support the Resolution.

In 1976 the Resolution achieved six per cent of the vote, the next year almost seven per cent. It was at the 1977 Annual General Meeting that the

Midland Chairman stated, in convoluted fashion, that the bank was not now making any loans to the South African government. The pressure may have had some part in this change of policy, although South Africa was also becoming an unsafe place to invest. ELTSA then turned its attention to the other British banks involved in Southern Africa: Barclays, the largest bank in that region; Standard Chartered, the second; and Hill Samuel, one of the largest organisers of much-needed loans for the apartheid regime.

Such campaigning of course continues to demand thousands of leaflets, endless efforts at publicity, permanent fund-raising, painstaking research, speaking, writing, phoning, persuading, encouraging, demanding. It is an existence whose unwilling devotees would gladly share with those whose cheerful parting shot — when you know they are *not* going to do what you've just asked them to do — is invariably 'So glad the Church has people like you to stir us up!'. The campaign reached perhaps its high point in an appearance before the United Nations Special Committee against Apartheid in June 1979. Supporters were encouraged, although none of the British United Nations staff bothered to turn up at the hearings. Possibly someone had told them that the Churches in Britain were doing their best not to be seen in public with these rather outspoken and controversial campaigning people and they had decided to do likewise. It perhaps goes without saying that, although ELTSA began as a Church-based campaign, it now draws much of its support from outside the Churches. The modern equivalent of *Matthew* 21, 31, may very well be that Marxists and communists will get into the Kingdom of God before those who believe they are God's elect.

This further stage of the campaign finally brought to light the basic disagreement between the Church financiers, like the Church Commissioners and the Methodist Central Finance Board, and those Christians who were pursuing the campaign in order to fight both racialism and oppressive economic and social structures. The loans were seen by the financiers merely as an unacceptable dimension of a system which was basically reformable by moral pressure. They certainly were not prepared to put investments at risk by supporting the withdrawal of banks from Southern Africa. The campaigners, Christian and non-Christian, believed that apartheid and the capitalist system were so basically intertwined that in order to destroy one, the other also had to be dismantled. The fundamental question for Christians then becomes a theological one, as to whether it is possible to accept capitalism as an economic system, with its inevitable social and political consequences, or whether the values of capitalism are so corrupting that the system itself has to be opposed.

The Principles

ELTSA's style, which has increasingly become one of confrontation, as banks continued to make loans and the Churches failed to offer a serious opposition, has produced some very illuminating theological experiences. To stand outside the imposing headquarters of international banks in the City of London, doing street theatre about how putting money into the South African 'piggy bank' always makes a profit, and facing the disinterest, the ridicule, the outright hostility of bank employees, is such an experience. To enter the Annual General Meeting of such a bank holding one share and to sit with those who hold thousands, even millions, to stand and put a question on South Africa and hear the shouts of 'communist', 'scroungers' and 'get back to work', is another. To go to Church financiers, who hold thousands – even millions – of Church people's shares, to plead with them for public commitment to stop all banking support for the apartheid system and to experience the paternalism, the excuses, the obeisance to 'charity law' and the eternal protestations of being on the same side really, that is yet another.

Such financiers, and the majority of the Church which supports them, are *not* on the same side as those with a radical political theology who work in groups like ELTSA. They support the status quo or, if necessary, a mild modification of it. They will sit down to lunch with a director whose company is profiting from and exploiting in Africa or Asia, but they will avoid if possible all direct contact with those whose communities are exploited. They offer no response to the Biblical challenge of transforming human society, a challenge which reflects the values of a Biblically-based understanding of mission and renewal, of crucifixion and resurrection. Christians who support campaigns such as ELTSA believe that it is the Church's Mission to be participating in the Kingdom of God; that to do that we need to get alongside the poor and the crucified; and that only from that perspective will we perceive the enormity of the task before us, which is to wipe out oppression and racism, to create the Kingdom where there is fellowship and freedom, equality of opportunity and peace, and to build a society in which each contributes according to ability and receives according to need.

The economic and political outworking of such a viewpoint is of course a socialist form of society, although it is recognised that no human society can hope to approach the reality of the Kingdom of God. Hence financial institutions, such as private banks, which live on the labour of others, are morally and theologically unacceptable.

Justification for action against economic and political powers who oppose the development of this form of society is very clearly found in the teaching and the activities of Amos, Micah, Isaiah and Jeremiah. There can be few more apposite Biblical passages concerning what the white

settlers have done to Southern Africa than Isaiah's parable of the
Vineyard (chap 5) and the prophet's warnings of death and destruction if
the Lord's voice is not heard (chap 6, vs 11-3) are surely already coming
true. It seems impossible to convince either Western Church financiers or
white South Africans of the relevance of this prophecy.

In the New Testament, one can look to Paul's teaching on how the
righteousness of God has superseded all demands of the law and on the
paramountcy of love and justice. Is it too much to ask that the Church,
instead of seeking desperately to avoid the task laid upon it as the
institution of discipleship by appealing to the law, should now expose
itself to the fearful and thrilling light of Calvary, where no law, no status,
no 'corporate fog' can hide the imperative of a Love which demands that
we 'do justice'? One can also look to Christ's teaching that it is the poor
who are blessed and that those who allow their wealth to become a barrier
to their discipleship are quite unable to follow Him, and that it is almost
impossible for a rich man to enter the Kingdom of God.

But then, why should rich and powerful bankers worry about what a
foolish and inconsequential religious teacher had to say two thousand
years ago? After all, he was crucified, wasn't he? Perhaps the main fault of
campaigning groups like ELTSA is that they operate much too carefully
within the rules ever to face crucifixion. But then it is hard to find any
Christian-based group in Britain today which is posing the fundamental
questions sharply enough really to challenge the principalities and powers.
Fortunately, Southern African blacks, Christian and otherwise, are made
of stronger stuff.

HISTORY

7. The Levellers and the English Democratic Tradition

Tony Benn

We are here today* to honour the memory of Private Church, Corporal
Perkins and Cornet Thompson – three English Levellers executed in
Burford churchyard in 1649 for their political activities; to recall the
beliefs of the Leveller movement of which they were members; to
consider the origins, development and contribution that that movement
has made to British democracy and socialism; and to discuss together in
the democratic manner of the Levellers themselves, the relevance of their
teaching to our society 327 years after their death.

The issues raised in the historic conflict between Charles I, resting his
claim to govern Britain on the Divine Right of Kings, and Parliament under
its Speaker, Lenthall, also a Burford man, which represented – albeit
imperfectly – a demand for the wider sharing of power, remain alive in
British politics to this day because they concern the use and abuse of state
power, which is a subject of universal and continuing relevance. But the
history we learned in our schools was not written to bring out, with equal
clarity, the underlying arguments about liberty and equality, and the role
of the Levellers who espoused them during those years of revolution. This
we are only now rediscovering for ourselves.

The Levellers grew out of the conditions of their own time. They
represented the aspirations of working people who suffered under the
persecution of kings, landowners and the priestly class, and they spoke for
those who experienced the hardships of poverty and deprivation. The
Levellers developed and campaigned, first with Cromwell and then against
him, for a political and constitutional settlement of the Civil War which
would embody principles of political freedom that anticipated by a
century and a half the main ideas of the American and French

---

* This is the text of an address given by Tony Benn on 15 May 1976 in Burford
Churchyard to commemorate the anniversary of the execution of three English
soldiers, members of the Leveller movement, in 1649.

Revolutions. The Levellers' advocacy of democracy and equality has been taken up by generations of liberal and socialist thinkers and activists, pressing for reforms, many of which are still strongly contested in our country to this day. The Levellers can now be seen not only as having played a major role in their own period, but as speaking for a popular liberation movement that can be traced right back to the teachings of the Bible and which has retained its vitality over the intervening centuries and which speaks to us here with undiminished force.

The Levellers found spokesmen and campaigners in John Lilburn, Richard Overton, William Walwyn, Gerrard Winstanley, the True Leveller or Digger, and others. These men were brilliant pamphleteers enjoying a shortlived freedom to print, publish and circulate their views at a time when censorship was temporarily in abeyance. They developed their own traditions of free discussion and vigorous petitioning and used them to formulate and advance their demands. These demands included the drafting of a major document called 'The Agreement of the People', which outlined a new and democratic constitution for Britain. The preamble to the third draft of this Agreement, published on 1 May 1649, runs as follows:

> 'We, the free People of England, to whom God hath given hearts, means and opportunity to effect the same, do with submission to his wisdom, in his name, and desiring the equity thereof may be to his praise and glory: Agree to ascertain our Government to abolish all arbitrary Power, and to set bounds and limits to our Supreme, and all Subordinate Authority, and remove all known Grievances.
> 'And accordingly to declare and publish to all the world, that we are agreed as followeth,
> '1. That the Supreme Authority of England and the Territories therewith incorporate, shall be and reside henceforward in a Representative of the people consisting of four hundred persons, but no more; in the choice of whom (according to natural right) all men of the age of one and twenty years and upwards (not being servants, or receiving alms, or having served in the late King in Arms or voluntary Contributions), shall have their voices.'

The Levellers held themselves to be free-born Englishmen, entitled to the protection of a natural law of human rights which they believed to originate in the will of God, rights vested in the people to whom alone true sovereignty belonged. These sovereign rights, the Levellers held, were only loaned to Parliament, to be elected on a wide popular franchise, which would hold them in trust. The Levellers also believed passionately in religious toleration and rejected oppression by presbyters as much as by priests, wishing to end the horrific record of executions, burnings, brandings and banishments that Christians had perpetrated on themselves and others that had led to the martyrdom of thousands of good Catholics and Protestants, non-conformists, dissenters, Jews and Gentiles alike.

The rank and file within the New Model Army spoke through Adjutants, Agents or Agitators (hence the special odium attaching to that word in the British establishment to this day) and they wore the sea-green colours that are still associated with incorruptibility. They demanded and won – for a time – democratic control of the Armed Forces and secured equal representations on a Grand Council of the Army sharing decisions with the Generals and Colonels, known to them as the Grandees. They regarded the Normans as oppressors of England and the King as the symbol of that Conquest who was buttressed and supported by land-owners who had seized much land once held in common, land that they argued should be restored to common ownership. They argued for universal state schools and hospitals to be provided at public expense three centuries before our generation began, so painfully, to construct the welfare state, the National Health Service and the comprehensive school system against so much resistance. The Levellers distilled their political philosophy, by discussion out of their own experience, mixing theory and practice, thought and action, and by doing so they passed on to succeeding generations a formula for social progress from which we can learn how to tackle the problems of our time. The Levellers won wide public support among the people as a whole and, although Cromwell and his generals ultimately defeated them, their ideas still retain a special place in the political traditions of the people of England.

Looking back on these ideas from the vantage point of the present, and knowing that they came out of the minds and experience of working people, few of whom enjoyed the formal education available today. It is impossible not to experience again the intense excitement and the controversy that those demands must have created when they were first formulated. It is also a real comfort for us to discover that, in our present social, political, human and industrial struggles, we are the inheritors of such a strong and ancient tradition of action and analysis.

The Levellers' debt to the Bible

Indeed to understand what the Levellers said and why, we must delve back far deeper into our own history. For the Levellers drew many of their ideas and much of their inspiration from the Bible, with its rich Jewish and Christian teaching. Critics of socialism often seek to dismiss socialism as being necessarily atheistical. But this is not true as far as British socialism is concerned. For the Bible has always been, and remains, a major element in our national political – as well as our religious –

education. And within our movement Christian Socialists have played an important role, along with Humanists, Marxists, Fabians and Co-operators.

The conflict in the Old Testament between the Kings and the Prophets — between temporal power and the preaching of righteousness — has greatly affected our own ideas about society; and of course lay at the heart of both arguments in the English Revolution, the one between the King and Parliament and the other one between Cromwell and the Levellers. For example, in the Bible it was the prophet Amos who said: 'But let judgement run down as waters and righteousness as a mighty stream' (*Amos* 5,24); and the Prophet Micah proclaimed the same message from God: 'He hath shewed thee O man what is good; and what doth the Lord require of thee, but to do justly, and to love mercy, and to walk humbly with thy God?' (*Micah* 6, 8).

Later, when Jesus Christ, the Carpenter of Nazareth, was asked by one of the scribes, 'What commandment is the first of all?', St Mark's Gospel, chapter 12, verses 29-31, records his answer. Jesus answered: 'The first is Hear O Israel; the Lord our God, the Lord is one: And thou shalt love the Lord thy God with all thy heart, and with all thy soul, and with all thy strength. The second is this, Thou shalt love thy neighbour as thyself. There is none other commandment greater than these.'

Jesus' classic restatement of the Old Testament teaching of Monotheism, and of brotherly love under one God which flowed from it, was absolutely revolutionary when uttered in a world which still accepted slavery. This passage also underlines the idea of man's relationship with God as a person-to-person relationship, neither needing nor requiring us to accept the intervention of an exclusive priestly class claiming a monopoly right to speak on behalf of the Almighty, still less of a King claiming a divine right to rule. These ideas lie at the root of religious dissent and gave birth to the idea of the priesthood of all believers which is central to non-conformity. H G Wells, himself a non-believer, writing of Jesus in his *History of the World,* recognised the revolutionary nature of Christ's teaching which led to his crucifixion:

'In view of what he plainly said, is it any wonder that all who were rich and prosperous felt a horror of strange things, a swimming of their world at his teaching? He was dragging out all the little private reservations they had made from social service into the light of a universal religious life. He was like some terrible moral huntsman digging mankind out of the snug burrows in which they had lived hitherto. In the white blaze of this kingdom of his there was to be no property, no privilege, no pride and precedence; no motive indeed and no reward but love. Is it any wonder that men were dazzled and blinded and cried out against him? Even his disciples cried out when he would not spare them the light. Is it any wonder that the priests realised that between this man and themselves there was no choice but that he or priestcraft should perish? Is it any wonder that the Roman soldiers, confronted and amazed by something soaring over their comprehension and threatening all their disciplines, should take refuge in wild laughter and crown him with thorns and robe him in purple and make a mock Caesar out of him? For to take him seriously was to enter upon a strange and alarming life, to abandon habits, to control instincts and impulses, to essay an incredible happiness.'

Wells' words must ranks as one of the most remarkable tributes to Christ ever to have come from a non-Christian.

Religious and political freedom

No wonder that many Bishops and clergy of the Church in England before the Reformation feared the Bible — if available to be widely read — might undermine the priestly hold over the minds of their flock. They therefore punished those like Wycliffe and the Lollards who translated the Bible into English and encouraged the people to read it, thus undermining the authority of the Bishops and the priesthood, the King and the landlords. In this same Church, here in Burford 120 years before the Levellers were shot, there was a gruesome example of the sort of punishment meted out to the Lollards.

The history of Oxfordshire tells us that a Burford Lollard paid £1 for an English Bible so that he could read it with his friends, many of them weavers. One of them, John Edmunds, told a Witney man 'to go offer his money to God's own image which was the poor people, blind and lame'. He and his followers were forced to kneel on the altar steps here in Burford church throughout the whole of the morning service in 1522, with faggots on their shoulders. These faggots were no doubt burned to heat the branding irons with which this group of Bible readers — 12 men and nine women — were all branded on the cheek at the end of prayers to teach the congregation not to read the Bible. For then, as now in many parts of the world, the Bible was seen as a revolutionary book, not to be trusted to the common people to read and interpret for themselves. It is no wonder that the Levellers should regard the Bible as their basic text.

The Leveller pamphlets abound with religious quotations. Divine teaching — as they read it — expressly prohibited the domination of man by man. One historian summarised the views being advanced by the lower classes at the beginning of the Civil Wars. This is what was being said, for example, in Chelmsford — and very radical it was:

'The relation of Master and Servant has no ground in the New

Testament; in Christ there is neither bond nor free. Ranks such as those of the peerage and gentry are ethnical and heathenish distinctions. There is no ground in nature or Scripture why one man should have £1,000 per annum, another not £1. The common people have been kept under blindness and ignorance, and have remained servants and slaves to the nobility and gentry. But God hath now opened their eyes and discovered unto them their Christian liberty.'

The Diggers, or True Levellers as they described themselves, went even further and in Gerrard Winstanley's pamphlet, *The True Levellers' Standard Advanced,* published on 26 April 1649, these words appear that anticipated the conservationists and commune dwellers of today, that denounced the domination of man by man, proclaimed the equality of women and based it all on God and Nature's laws:

'In the beginning of Time, the great Creator, Reason, made the Earth to be a common Treasury, to preserve Beasts, Birds, Fishes and Man, the lord that was to govern this Creation; for Man had Domination given to him, over the Beasts, Birds and Fishes; but not one word was spoken in the beginning that one branch of mankind should rule over another.
'And the reason is this, every single man, Male and Female, is a perfect creature of himself; and the same Spirit that made the Globe dwells in man to govern the Globe; so that the flesh of man being subject to Reason, his Maker, hath him to be his Teacher and Ruler within himself, therefore needs not run abroad after any Teacher and Ruler without him, for he needs not that any man should teach him, for the same Anoynting that ruled in the Son of Man, teacheth him all things.
'But since humane flesh (that king of Beasts) began to delight himself in the objects of the Creation, more than in the Spirit Reason and Righteousness ... Covetousness, did set up one man to teach and rule over another; and thereby the Spirit was killed, and man was brought into Bondage and became a greater Slave to such of his own kind than the Beasts of the field were to him.
'And hereupon the Earth (which was made to be a Common Treasury for relief for all, both Beasts and Men) was hedged in to Inclosures by the teachers and rulers, and the others were made Servants and Slaves; And that Earth that is within this Creation made a Common Store-house for all, is bought and sold, and kept in the hands of a few, whereby the great Creator is mightly dishonoured, as if He were a respecter of persons, delighting in the comfortable livelihood of some, and rejoycing in the miserable povertie and straights of others. From the beginning it was not so.'

The plain advocacy of absolute human equality — and the emphasis on the common ownership of land and natural resources, speak to us today with the same power as when those words were written by Winstanley.

The Bridge between Christianity and Socialism

But some Levellers went beyond the authority of the Bible and began to develop out of it, and from their own experience, a humanist buttress for their social philosophy without losing its moral force. The Levellers were, in a special sense, bridge-builders; constructing a bridge that connects Christian teaching with humanism and democratic socialism. Those who crossed that bridge did not blow it up behind them as converts to atheism might have done. That bridge is still there for anyone who wishes to cross it in either direction. Some use it to go back to trace one of the paths leading to the Bible. Others, like the modern Christian pilgrims — for example, the Catholic priests and others in Latin America — whose experience of modern world poverty, persecution and oppression has spurred them on to cross that same bridge from Christianity to social action and democratic socialism, have based it on their Christian faith, and the inspiration of saintly Christians who have pioneered along the same path.

The moral force of Bible teaching and the teachings of Jesus are not necessarily weakened by being secularised. Indeed it can be argued that humanism may entrench them more strongly for those who cannot accept the Christian faith. Christians believe that the Almighty created man to be his children and that the brotherhood of man, under God, is the basis of all social morality, and divine source of authority for it. Humanists by contrast, accepting the brotherhood of man as a deeply felt experience, explain the idea of a Divine Father as deriving from man's desire to embody his highest aspirations of social morality in that reverent way through a personal God. Though these beliefs stand in blank opposition to each other, theologically, many Christians, humanists and secular socialists are, in practice, committed to a code of human ethics that is intended to be identical in its application to society, however far below this ideal man may fall in practice. A similar unity of apparent opposites may be seen in comparing the negative and positive of a photograph. These differ sharply in that black and white appear to be transposed. But the picture itself is the same when projected onto a screen, depending on the light source used.

But however we choose to explain this theological paradox, Christian, Humanist and Socialist morality have, in fact, co-existed and co-operated throughout history and they co-exist and co-operate today most fruitfully and not only within the Christian Socialist movement itself. The British Trade Union and Labour movement, like Anglicans, Presbyterians,

Catholics, Methodists, Congregationalists, Baptists, Jews and campaigners for civil rights have all gained inspiration from these twin traditions of Christianity and Humanistic socialism. We should certainly not allow the horrors of persecution perpetrated at various times in history by societies proclaiming themselves to be Christian to blind us to the true social morality of socialism.

We owe a deep debt of gratitude to the Levellers for building that bridge and for defending the people from the abuses of power of which some priests and commissars may be equally guilty because they falsely claim to be the interpreters of some truth revealed solely to them. The pure and principled stance of the Levellers on these matters explains the survival of their ideas.

The inheritance left by the Levellers

The ideas of the Levellers were thought to be so dangerous because of their popularity then that, as now, the establishment wanted to silence them. By 1650 the Levellers' movement had been effectively crushed. Cromwell's Commonwealth represented a formidable advance compared to the reign of King Charles which preceded it. But it did not — and in terms of its historical and industrial development probably could not — adopt the principles that Lilburn, Overton and Walwyn, still less Winstanley, were advocating. Ten years later came the Restoration of Charles II.

In 1688 Britain witnessed the shadowy beginnings of a Constitutional Monarchy which, as it emerged at the time, had practically nothing whatever in common with real political democracy. But the elimination of the Levellers as an organised political movement could not obliterate the ideas which they had propagated. From that day to this, the same principles of religious and political freedom and equality have reappeared again and again in the history of the Labour movement and throughout the world. The American colonists inscribed these principles clearly in their Declaration of Independence issued by the Congress on 4 July 1776:

> 'We hold these Truths to be self-evident that all Men are created equal, that they are endowed by their Creator with certain inalienable Rights, that among these are Life, Liberty and the Pursuit of Happiness. That to secure these Rights Governments are instituted among Men deriving their just Powers from the Consent of the Governed.'

The document was drafted by our American cousins but the ideas were taken straight from the English Levellers a century and a quarter before. The Americans had also drawn heavily on the writings of Tom Paine, who was a direct heir of the Leveller tradition and whose *Rights of Man* also won him a place in the history of the French Revolution where, although English, he was elected as a Deputy to the first French Constituent Assembly summoned to implement the principles of 'Liberty, Equality and Fraternity'.

The English reformers of the early nineteenth century also drew many of their ideas from that mysterious mix of Christian teaching, religious and political dissent, social equality and democracy. This fired the imagination of generations of Congregationalists, trade union pioneers, early Co-operators, socialists and the Chartists who also used language which the Levellers themselves might have spoken. We can find the same aspiration in the moving words of Clause Four written in 1918, which set out the objectives of the Labour Party in a positive way, thus:

'To secure for the workers by hand or brain the full fruits of their industry and the most equitable distribution thereof that may be possible upon the basis of the common ownership of the means of production, distribution and exchange and the best obtainable system of popular administration and control of each industry or service. 'Generally to promote the Political, Social and Economic Emancipation of the People and more particularly of those who depend directly upon their own exertions by hand or brain for the means of life.'

The same ideas are expressed in the present commitment of the Labour movement: 'To bring about a fundamental and irreversible shift in the balance of wealth and power in favour of working people and their families.' The massive impetus of these ideas with variations deriving from their own traditions, have influenced all the working peoples of the world who are a part of this same movement, uniting those once separated by barriers of narrow nationalism but all facing degrading poverty, deprivation and persecution.

The Levellers and today

If the Levellers were here today they might be surprised to find so much attributed to their movement which, for them, must have seemed to have ended in abject failure. They would be pleased at such progress as we have made since 1649 but, being analysts of the nature of society, they would also see that much of the power structure within the social and political system has survived unscathed despite the outward appearance of reform. What would the Levellers say to us if they were here today? I hope the question will start a debate and lead to a fuller examination of the nature of our present society. For my part I think the Levellers would have much to say about the issues which concern us here in England in 1976 — and I have selected ten issues which I believe would concern them.

☐ The Levellers would surely concentrate their attention on the huge accumulation of financial power in our society and the continued exclusion of working people from effective democratic power over it, and link the present maldistribution of wealth here and worldwide to the maldistribution of power. They would champion all those in Britain and throughout the world who experience poverty.

☐ The Levellers would view with deep suspicion the power of the military establishments to be found worldwide, sometimes incorporating political police forces which seem to believe that they have a divine right to secrecy served by a network of spies and agents, using bribery and corruption to serve their purposes without regard to moral principles.

☐ The Levellers would immediately see the relevance of industrial democracy, by workers' control or self-management, as a natural extension of the political franchise to replace the power of the new industrial feudalism which has long established itself through the growth of giant companies. If the Levellers were to describe shop stewards, in this context, as 'agitators', they would be restoring an ancient and honourable word to its proper meaning just as each Sunday Anglicans pray for the 'whole state of Christ's Church militant here on earth' — despite the popular odium now attaching to all 'militants'.

☐ The Levellers might see in the immense influence of the educational establishment, under the titular leadership of the universities, a new class of rulers in a self-perpetuating hierarchy, aiming to establish a claim to the 'private ownership of knowledge' which by rights is the 'common store house' belonging to us all.

☐ The Levellers might see in the mass media a modern secular church seeking to control the minds of the people by standard sermons from television pulpits, day after day and night after night, keeping out dissenters or spokesmen for the common people, imposing a technical monopoly censorship that frustrates the right to free speech because it denies the equally important right to be heard.

☐ The Levellers would uphold the right of constituents to recall and replace their Parliamentary candidates, on the same basis and for the same reason as dissenting chapels claimed the right to appoint and dismiss their Ministers, and because of the inalienable sovereignty of the people which no Parliament has any right to usurp. I imagine that, for the same reason, they would deeply suspect the law-making powers of the Brussels Commissioners who are not accountable to electors with powers to remove them.

☐ The Levellers, and still more the Diggers, would add a new and moral dimension to the movement for conserving the earth's limited resources by reminding man of his duty to his fellow citizens and his descendants, not to squander the earth's 'Common Treasury' because it is God's gift to each generation in turn, a powerful argument for common ownership and a classless society.

☐ The Levellers would demand a far greater public accountability by all those who exercise centralised civil, political, scientific, technical, educational and mass power, through the bureaucracies of the world, and would call for the democratic control of it all.

☐ The Levellers would warn against looking for deliverance to any elite group, whatever its origins, even if it came from the Labour movement, who might claim some special ability to carry through reforms by proxy, free from the discipline of recall or re-election. They would argue that all real reform comes from below, and that the self-confidence of the common people in organising for themselves — in their unions, trades, crafts, local communities and civil and human rights groups, enlarging their own horizons by their own efforts, distilling their own wisdom from their own experience and breeding their own collective leadership in the process, offered the only real guarantee of advance.

☐ The Levellers would argue passionately for free speech and make common cause, worldwide, with those who fight for human rights against tyrants and dictators of all political colours, not sparing Stalinists who falsely seek to justify uniformity as a necessary defence for socialism.

To summarise all those lessons, the one connecting thread that united the Levellers to each other and that unites us to them is a passion for democracy advocated for moral and practical reasons, both because it recognises the rights of man, and because democracy imposes responsibilities on those who exercise those rights. True the Levellers believed in original sin. But for them the most dangerous sin was the corruption of political power for personal gain. They would have reconciled the problem of entrusting responsibility through the ballot box to a people prone to sin, in the same way that Dr Rheinhold Niebuhr, the American theologian, did when he defended democracy in these words:

'Man's capacity for evil makes democracy necessary.
Man's capacity for good makes democracy possible.'

I say the Levellers would do and say all these things were they here
amongst us. But, given the power of their ideas to move us, even today, in
what sense can we say that they are not here?

8. The Christian Left in Britain (1850-1950)

Ken Leech

The description 'Christian Socialist' has been applied to a diverse range of movements and tendencies. The jibe that it combined reformist socialism with heretical Christianity is undoubtedly true of some, but not all, of its manifestations. In fact the history of the 'Christian Left' since the early 1850s is complex and includes many conflicting elements.

The importance of Frederick Denison Maurice (1805-1872) is difficult to overstate. It was from the movement of thought initiated by Maurice, J M Ludlow (1821-1911), Charles Kingsley (1819-1875) and others between 1848 and 1855 that the notion of 'Christian Socialism' emerged, the term first being used in the *Tracts on Christian Socialism* of 1850. It is true to say that 'the Christian "Socialist" school was not really Socialist' or that its socialism was 'of a rather dubious variety'. Certainly they wished to remove the injustices of industrial society by voluntary cooperative enterprise. Their movement was in its origin a reaction to Chartism, a movement which also was not socialist but which contained some radical Christian elements. 'I am a Church of England clergymen,' cried Kingsley at a public meeting, 'and I am a Chartist.' However, in contrast to the Chartists, the Christian Socialists opposed universal suffrage and supported the union of Church and state. Maurice claimed that 'confused, disorderly notions' were stirring up the Chartists and socialists, and in 1848 he offered his services as a special constable to help put down the expected Chartist rising. He feared anarchy, regarded Owenism and Chartism as dangerous and wished to 'Christianise' the Chartist movement. So the Christian Socialists issued their series *Politics for the People.*

The thinking of this group was greatly influenced by French ideas of cooperative production. Maurice pointed out that 'the socialism I speak of is that of Owen, Fourier, Louis Blanc — of the Englishmen, Frenchmen, Germans, who have fraternised with them or produced systems of their own'. But Maurice was no socialist in the later sense. He condemned the sovereignty of the people as atheistic and subversive, believed that democracy led to slavery, and preferred monarchy. Kingsley held that 'a landed aristocracy was a blessing to the country and that no country would gain the highest liberty without such a class'. Ludlow, a disciple of Blanc, knew more about socialism than Maurice did. A contemporary commented:

> 'J M Ludlow was the main-spring of our Christian Socialist Movement. Maurice and the rest knew nothing about Socialism. Ludlow, educated in Paris, knew all. He got us round Maurice and really led us.'[1]

So, while Maurice applied the term socialist to himself in 1850, the outlook of his group was more Tory paternalist: 'their approach to the working class was one of condescending, though quite honest, benevolence'.

> '... they never joined "the Movement", they never marched with the working class. There is no evidence that they ever read a single word of Marx and the chief thing that has to be grasped about them is that their significance does not lie in the political sphere at all.'[2]

Even Father Adderley, writing in 1910, distinguished 'Christian Socialism' from 'our thoroughgoing socialism'. Referring to Maurice and Kingsley, he wrote that 'neither of these great men were socialist: they were not even democrats'.

But the theology of Maurice, with its stress on the glory of man, its classical view of the atonement, and its understanding of human unity as grounded in the doctrine of the Trinity, was of fundamental importance for the later developments in socialist Christian thought.

In Britain, from the Chartist period there had been a trend which connected political demands with Christianity. One Chartist newspaper advised its readers to 'study the New Testament: it contains all the elements of Chartism'. Later the Labour movement as it evolved contained many persons of marked Christian outlook. Keir Hardie saw socialism as the dethronement of Mammon, and Ramsey McDonald's opposition to capitalism was based on the fact that it was anti-Christian. In the early twentieth century there were numerous attempts in Liberal Protestantism to establish a correspondence between Christianity and socialism. Much of this thinking was influenced by the 'social gospel' school. Walter Rauschenbusch (1886-1918) provided the basis for a theology of the Kingdom of God on earth which he interpreted to mean the progressive regeneration of human society by the Spirit of Christ. In 1912

Rauschenbusch could claim that 'the largest and hardest part of the work of Christianising the social order has been done'.[3]

The emergence of an explicitly political movement among Anglicans occurred towards the end of the nineteenth century. It was the Guild of St Matthew, founded at Bethnal Green in 1877 by Stewart Headlam (1847-1924), which first incorporated the idea of common ownership of land into the basis of its programme. It would be entirely wrong to see Headlam as typical of the Tractarian movement or of its 'slum priests', for 'on the whole Catholics in the Church of England have been apolitical'.

'The Tractarians, despite their theological revolt against evangelicalism, still saw the poor as individual souls to be saved, and not as members of a society to be transformed.'[4]

It may be that there was an implicit social theology in the Oxford Movement. But in Headlam were found two unusual and uncomfortable viewpoints. First, he agreed with Maurice and Pusey when they admitted that they worshipped different Gods — and Headlam's God was the God of Maurice. But, secondly, Headlam held that Maurice's theology was incomplete unless it was embodied in sacramental worship.

Headlam's views on politics, the theatre, pubs, biblical criticism and ritual shocked many churchmen, and he was poles apart from the mainstream Tractarians. Yet he taught the Athanasian Creed to working class atheistic followers of Charles Bradlaugh and insisted that 'a Socialist is not doing his best for the spread of Socialism unless he is a thorough Catholic Churchman'. He saw the Church as 'the community which Jesus Christ founded', stressed indiscriminate baptism as an essential aspect of the egalitarian nature of the Church, and saw the Eucharist as the archetype of a new world order.

'We have from the beginning in this Guild, and rightly, connected the restoration of the Mass to its proper place with our secular and political work: our sacramentalism with our socialism ... we are socialists because we are sacramentarians.'[5]

The Guild of St Matthew (GSM) reached its peak in the 1890s with 99 clergy and 265 lay members, but afterwards it declined and in 1909 Headlam wound it up.

It was Frederick Verinder who, more than any single other person, gave to the Guild a biblical basis for its concern with land. Verinder pointed out that the Mosaic Law was hostile to the whole development of the landlord system. 'The principle which underlies the Mosaic agrarian legislation is absolutely fatal to what we know as landlordism. Jehovah is the only landlord; the land is his because he and none other created it: all men are his tenants.'[6]

So the Guild became increasingly dominated by the question of land, and Headlam became a disciple of the economist Henry George. Yet it was to the Scriptures that Headlam appealed for the Guild's stress on the land issue. When on 20 June 1886 Queen Victoria began her Jubilee Year, the Guild's journal *Church Reformer* celebrated it with these words:

> 'The Queen's Jubilee is good; but the People's Jubilee is better. Why may not the year upon which we now enter be the Jubilee of both Queen and People? For the Jubilee of the Hebrews, as ordained by the great statesman whom God for their deliverance raised up and inspired, was the Jubilee of a whole People; and its observance was founded upon, and was expressly designed to conserve, a divinely ordained system of Land Nationalisation.'[7]

As well as Headlam, two other Guild members whose contribution was very considerable were Charles Marson (1859-1914) and Thomas Hancock (1832-1903). Marson was the author of *God's Cooperative Society,* while Hancock's sermons are a little-known but invaluable source for the theology of the sacramental socialism of this era. It was Hancock who coined the famous phrase 'the banner of Christ in the hands of the socialists' and called the Magnificat 'the hymn of the universal social revolution'.

What we find in the theology of Headlam and his colleagues in the GSM is the fusion of Maurician theology with sacramentalism and ritualism. 'The new Christian Socialism,' to use Adderley's term, had moved far beyond Maurice, but Adderley saw the GSM as representing a further stage which he called 'Church Socialism'. Yet it has often been claimed that Headlam's politics were 'really those of Liberal Fabianism'. Certainly he remained a member of the Liberal Party until his death, and he attacked attempts to create an Independent Labour Party. His dependence on George too caused many to dispute his socialism, for George was no socialist in spite of his concern with the land tax. But Headlam was not an orthodox Georgite, and he argued for socialisation of capital as well as land. His support for the Liberal Party was due to the fact that he held that unless Liberal values were preserved, a socialist order might contain similar evils to those within capitalism. But no one who has studied Headlam's writings can be in serious doubt as to his socialism and its theological foundations.

Unlike the GSM, the Christian Social Union, founded in 1889 by Charles Gore, Henry Scott Holland and others, was never really socialist, though it was strongly opposed to unbridled individualism. Its influence

on Bishops, on the Lambeth Conferences and on the mainstream thinking
of Anglicanism was very considerable. By the turn of the century it had
6,000 members. B F Westcott (1815-1901), Bishop of Durham and a
disciple of Maurice, was one of the leading biblical scholars of his day and
a leading thinker of the CSU. In his famous address to the Church
Congress of 1890, Westcott used the word 'socialism' to describe a way of
life, and he contrasted it with individualism, which he associated with
evangelical Christianity. Similarly the Lambeth Conferences from 1888 to
1908 were very concerned with socialist issues and very critical of laissez-
faire economics. The 1920 Conference specifically called for 'fundamental
change' in economic life. But, as Reckitt, writing of the background to the
thought of P E T Widdrington, noted, the word 'socialism' was not being
used in a very clear political sense.

'The word was being accepted as a description which adherents of an
"evolutionary" interpretation of the associative principle in human
society were ready to adopt as an indication of their revolt against a
rapacious, irresponsible and at this date a notably unsuccessful
economic system.'[8]

The chief importance of the CSU was at two levels: first, that of its
concern with specific social evils such as the adulteration of goods,
misleading accounts of their quality, sweating and so on. But, secondly,
that of its theological work in creating a framework in which socialist
thought could develop within Christian circles. One of its leading
theologians was Charles Gore (1853-1932), founder of the Community of
the Resurrection. Gore's writings had a tremendous influence on Anglican
thought, and the symposium *Lux Mundi* (1889) which he edited has been
seen as having an importance in relation to Christian socialism comparable
to that of *Fabian Essays* in relation to British socialism as a whole. While
the volume did not advocate socialism, its implications were clearly in that
direction.

In 1906 a group of Anglo-Catholic clergy met at Morecambe and
formed the Church Socialist League. The leaders of this group were Lewis
Donaldson, W E Moll, Conrad Noel and Percy Widdrington. Many of the
members felt that the Labour Party was too reformist. The aim of the
CSL was 'the establishment of a democratic commonwealth in which the
community shall own the land and capital collectively, and use them
cooperatively for the good of all'. Donaldson described the aims of the
League as follows:

'The Church Socialist League was originated to affirm the essential
parts of Socialism as necessary inferences from the Christian faith:

pity for the weak, justice for the oppressed, the inviolable sanctity of
every individual life as an end in itself, and fellowship instead of
competition as the dominant method in industry and commerce,
issuing in the idea of corporate possession of the means of life, as
nobler than that of "private" ownership.'[9]

But there was a tension between those who wanted the CSL to concentrate
on theology and those who wanted it to move more into political action.
In 1912 it rejected a proposal that it should affiliate to the Labour Party
and in 1912 Widdrington persuaded it to concentrate on theology.
Widdrington held that the contemporary socialism was too relative and
that the need was to develop a 'Christian sociology'. On the other hand,
Conrad Noel, the organising secretary of the CSL, had preferred the
League to the CSU because the latter, he complained, 'gloried in its
indefiniteness, considered it a crime to come to any economic conclusion...
ever learning, never coming to the truth.'
    The years after the First World War saw the emergence of a number of
bodies and tendencies – the Archbishops' Committee's Fifth Report on
Christianity and Industrial Problems, published in 1918, the Conference
on Christian Politics, Economics and Citizenship (COPEC) in 1921, and so
on. It was from COPEC that the concept of a 'Christian sociology' became
established in theological usage.

'Far from agreeing with those who declare that there can be no such
thing as a Christian sociology or Christian economics, we would urge
that it is only in so far as the scientific study of the problems of man's
corporate life takes account of the revelation in Christ and of the power
manifested by him, that it is true to human nature and that its
conclusions are worthy of respect.'[10]

In 1923, 510 Anglican priests signed a memorial to Ramsay McDonald,
congratulating the Labour Party on becoming the official opposition and
promising support. The organiser of this was Lewis Donaldson (1860-
1953), Canon of Peterborough and later of Westminster. It was Donaldson
who coined the phrase 'Christianity is the religion of which socialism is
the practice'. He had been a curate to H C Shuttleworth, a leading member
of the GSM, and had been Chairman of the CSL until 1916.
    With the disbanding of the CSL in 1923, two new groups emerged, the
Society of Socialist Christians and the League of the Kingdom of God.
The SSC was an interdenominational body which affiliated to the Labour
Party. The LKG was formed by Widdrington and was not a socialist body,
though most of its members were socialists. The League held that 'the
Catholic faith demands a challenge to the world by the repudiation of

capitalist plutocracy and the wage system, and stands for a social order in which the means of life subserve the commonwealth'. In 1922 an important symposium, *The Return of Christendom,* was published which argued the case for Catholic sociology based on distributed property, the just price, and the guild system. This volume paved the way for a good deal of subsequent work towards the idea of a Christian society. It contained a paper by Maurice Reckitt, soon to become the principal historian of the modern Christian social movement, on the idea of 'Christendom' in modern society, and one from Widdrington on 'The return of the Kingdom of God'. It was this paper which introduced the theme of the Kingdom as 'the regulative principle of theology'. The League of the Kingdom of God avoided any direct commitment to socialism and, unlike the CSL, it omitted references to common ownership.

Out of the 1922 symposium and the League came the Christendom Group, which Reckitt described in 1947 as 'the strongest nucleus of Christian sociological thinking'. From 1931 the Group issued the journal *Christendom,* edited by Widdrington. It also set up the Anglo-Catholic Summer School of Sociology which met at Oxford from 1925. It was a remarkable group which stressed the origins of Catholic social thought in Catholic dogma and favoured a reformed financial system and a guild organisation for industry. Egerton Swann defined the three central ideas of Catholic sociology as distributed property, just price and the guild system. The economic thought of Christendom, however, became linked with the Social Credit theories of C H Douglas, though the Group was not committed to Social Credit as is sometimes claimed.

The Christendom Group has been heavily criticised. Thus the economist, D L Munby, wrote of them:

> 'What characterised the writings of this group was a brilliance of intellect and imaginative grasp of problems unhampered by any solid knowledge of the realities of the issues with which they tried to grapple, and any willingness to learn from experts. As a result they naturally failed to say anything of significance on economic matters.'[11]

Evans, in a substantial history of the Christian social tradition with a strong socialist outlook, significantly failed to mention them at all. His colleague, Kenneth Ingram, however, claimed that their critique of financial industrialism was a 'pre-capitalist not post-capitalist criticism'.

Nevertheless, the influence of this Group on the Church was a major one. It is probably from the Christendom period that the now well-established use of the term 'technological' as a (pejorative) description of our society comes, and their critique of what Philip Mairet called 'a

civilisation of Technics' spread to the Amsterdam Assembly which set up
the World Council of Churches in 1948. During the 1930s and '40s there
was a spate of writing on Christianity and social change, with titles such as
*Catholicism and the Need for Revolution, The Red Bible, Towards the
Christian Revolution* and *The Economics of the Kingdom of God.* The
high water mark of the period was the Malvern Conference of 1941,
followed in 1942 by the publication of William Temple's *Christianity and
the Social Order,* and by the Conference on Politics, Economics and
Citizenship (COPEC). Temple's book sold 130,000 copies and his
writings were perhaps the major influence on mainstream Anglican
thinking in this period. Temple (1881-1944) was Archbishop of York
from 1929 to 1942 and of Canterbury from 1942-1944. But Temple was
not a socialist. He supported private ownership provided it was not
exploitive and he followed Keynesian ideas, arguing for 'withering capital'.
As Stanley Evans wrote of him in 1944:

> 'He is not a socialist. Economically he stands for a planned capitalism,
> and has some sort of hankering for "guilds" and "corporativism": he
> himself is a democrat, although, if carried out, his theories might lead
> in another direction.'[12]

To see the way in which a more distinctly socialist tradition grew up in
contrast to the Christendom tradition, it is necessary to return to the
period of the Church Socialist League. It was because of his
disillusionment with the League that Conrad Noel (1869-1942) founded
the Catholic Crusade. The Crusade, based at Thaxted in Essex, stood for
'a revolutionary attitude in politics, and the establishment, if necessary by
force, of a classless cooperative society on communist lines'. It described
itself as a company of people who accept 'the *whole* Catholic faith' and
therefore seek to set up the Kingdom of God on earth. They saw the
Kingdom as 'a Commonwealth which in economics, politics, art and
recreation shall be the outward and visible expression of God — the Spirit
of Justice, Comradeship and Freedom'. Because the present world-order,
with imperialism, land-monopoly, and Mammon-worship was the outward
expression of greed, injustice and oppression, the Crusade set out to
expose its wickedness and seek its destruction.

The Noel movement was 'fundamentally opposed' to modern Papalism
and to conventional Anglo-Catholicism, though Jack Bucknall said that it
represented the synthesis of all that was best in the Anglo-Catholic revival.
Etienne Watts held that 'it was the intention of the leaders of the Oxford
Movement to restore to the Church in England a true Christian ideology in
place of the Erastianism which obtained in their time' and so 'the future
of the Oxford Movement is bound up in an intensive extension of Catholic

doctrine along the lines of realist Christian social revolution and reconstruction'. Noel's theology was deeply Incarnational and sacramental. He wrote in 1933:

> 'It is necessary for the beginner to grasp this conviction about the nature of God and of Man if he is to understand our idea of sacraments, of authority, of civil government, of politics, and economics. The Catholic Crusade philosophy is all of a piece. It will change your views on music, on decoration, on the colour of a piece of material, equally with your views of man's end, the reading of history and the revolution.'[13]

Noel opposed the repressive elements in Catholicism, wrote of 'the revolutionary significance' of apostolic succession and hoisted the Red Flag in Thaxted Church. He saw ritual as subversive: the Holy Sacrament was 'a foretaste of the world to come' and 'of the Common production and distribution of bread and pleasure in the International Commonwealth of God and of his Righteousness'.

The collapse of the Crusade was closely connected with the Stalin-Trotsky dispute. Reg Groves, the historian both of the origins of British Trotskyism and of the Catholic Crusade, has described the early growth of a Trotskyist movement in Britain. In his notes to the Crusade Manifesto he comments:

> 'From 1929 onwards, the poison of Stalinism was being injected into all left-wing groups; and members of the Crusade were infected, some of them incurably. Factional disputes disrupted the Crusade in the thirties, as they disrupted all other left-wing groups. After prolonged and bitter discussion, John and Mary Groser and the group at Christ Church, Watney Street, Stepney, were driven out of the Crusade in March 1932.'[14]

John Groser became one of the best-known figures in the socialist movement in the East End, being President of Stepney Tenants' Defence League and playing a major role in anti-fascist activity in the '30s. Groser and Jack Bucknall were curates together in Poplar from 1922-25, and in the early '30s Bucknall was writing strongly pro-Trotsky articles in the *Catholic Crusader:*

> 'Trotsky calls himself Atheist, but if while denying a Creator of the Universe, he yet asserts by his life and work Eternal Goodness, Truth and Beauty which are God's character, he will help in the building of the Kingdom of God. Stalin and the Stalinised Communists of today

have done great work, but if their Atheism is self-satisfied, so that by their conduct they deny their eternal principles, any society based on such a denial must come to irreparable disaster. We are at a crisis in the history of the race. If there is a voice crying in the wilderness, we must have ears to hear. It may not be accidental that Trotsky is a Jew. It may be that he is in line with the great Jewish Prophets of the ages. If so we should do well to take heed — for salvation is of such Jews.'[15]

However, other Crusaders took a different line, and it was the attitude to the Soviet Union which finally led to the disbanding of the Crusade in 1937 and its transformation for a while into the Order of the Church Militants (OCM). The theological emphasis of the OCM was identical with that of the Crusade, for Noel was still the principal theologian. The Order expressed its concern to 'revive the whole Catholic Faith especially remembering such articles of it as have been neglected'. There was the stress on the Trinity, on the Incarnation and on 'Christ's International Commonwealth', as well as encouragement for 'the mass pacifism of the sympathetic strike' and opposition to fascism and militarism. Its attitude to capitalism was simple and direct. 'The present industrial system, being based on the mortal sin of avarice, and enslaving the people by means of rents, interest and wagery, must be destroyed at the roots and a new order built.'

The OCM held summer schools at Thaxted on such themes as 'Liturgy and Life' and 'Worship and the World Revolution'. In 1939 it was involved in the debate on the Popular Front, with Bucknall holding that the only hope lay in re-forming the International Party.

It is often said that Noel was an uncritical Stalinist. But in his review of Boris Souvarine's *Stalin* (1939) he concluded that Trotsky was more idealistic and more loyal to the ultimate goals of world communism. Stalin, however, was a superb tactician who could outwit fascism with its own weapons. How Noel's thought would have developed is a matter for speculation, but in 1942 he died, and soon the organised movement which he had founded ceased to exist. However, it was around the issue of Stalinism and of Soviet Marxism that the divisions in the Christian Left of the '40s and '50s were to focus.

The Council of Clergy and Ministers for Common Ownership, set up in the early 1940s, saw the capitalist system as 'immoral and unChristian...a worship of Mammon...plainly a work of the devil'. It later became the Society of Socialist Clergy and Ministers and issued a journal, *Magnificat.* Soon the intellectual leadership of the SSCM fell to Stanley Evans (1912-1965) and in his period foreign affairs became dominant. Evans was the *Daily Worker* correspondent at the trial of Cardinal Mindszenty and one of the leaders of the British Soviet Friendship Society. During the 1940s he edited *Religion and the People* which carried a continuous critique of the social record of the Churches and was a major source, sometimes the only source, for accurate information on Eastern Europe. After 1956 Evans edited *Junction,* a journal of 'Anglican realism' – which continued till his death in 1965. Evans was an influential theologian, steeped in patristics as well as in Marxism, and his thought was dominated by the vision of the Kingdom of God on earth. In 1954 he was pointing to a 'crisis in Christian thought' marked by social pessimism and hopelessness.

The other group which was formed after the disappearance of the CSL in 1923, the Society of Socialist Christians, merged into the Socialist Christian League in 1932 and was linked to the Labour Party, although it contained members who continued the Guild Socialist tradition of G D H Cole. R H Tawney was its President. In 1960 the SSCM and the SCL merged to form the Christian Socialist Movement.

The late 1950s was a time of crisis and confusion. The Christian Left, like the secular Left, was profoundly shaken by the 20th Congress of the Soviet Communist Party, with its revelations about the Stalin period, and by the events in Hungary. Many left the British Communist Party, and the 'New Left' emerged from a fusion of the dissident *Reasoner* and the Universities and Left Review group. Within the Christian Socialist Movement, Stanley Evans, who had, only three years earlier, preached a glowing memorial sermon for Stalin, wrote *Russia Reviewed* (1956) in which he confessed that 'most of us who have written and spoken about Russia and Eastern Europe, while we have reported truly and gauged accurately some aspects of Soviet life, and the life of the New Democracies, have been grievously wrong about others'. He went on:

'However admirable may be the economic and the moral basis of a social system – and the Soviet idea of ownership is both economically and morally sound – there is no limit to the mistakes, the follies and the crimes which can be perpetrated within it. Approval of a social system cannot be an alternative to constant vigilance as to how it develops and what goes on within it.'[16]

The movement of intellectuals out of the Communist Party as a result of the experience of Stalinism has tended to be seen mainly as a movement to the Right. To some extent this was true among the Christians, but it was not wholly true. Many remained on the Left and have continued to play significant roles in the '60s and '70s. By the end of the '50s, however, the organised Christian Left was in disarray. Much of the theological dynamic of the earlier movements had gone. In the mid-50s there was little serious Christian social thinking, and Michael Ramsey was complaining in 1955 that 'Christian sociology' was under the weather.

Some small groups were meeting: an American Order, the Society of the Catholic Commonwealth, had a small cell in the East End of London and combined Thomist philosophy with Marxist analysis, while nearby the Christian Anarchists were meeting at Bow Common. But the movements of Christian social and political thought were not to re-emerge until the '60s and early '70s. In 1960 Ronald Preston wrote of 'the Christian Left still lost' and of 'the irrelevance of much of the traditional thought of the Christian Left'. Today many young socialist Christians are unaware of much of the thinking and activity of the past. But Reg Groves's words about the Catholic Crusade are applicable over a much wider area:

'More than half a century separates us from that obscure April day in 1918 when a handful of people founded the Catholic Crusade. The golden lads and girls are old, or have, as chimney sweepers, come to dust. Little that is tangible remains, only a fragment of the dream held in the words of the Manifesto. Contemplating the baseness of spirit infecting increasingly our culture and our common life, the savage exploitation and destruction of our natural resources, and the behaviour of the modern reprobates of socialism and communism, what the Manifesto of the Catholic Crusade tried to say grows, not diminishes, in wisdom amd relevance as the years roll by.'[17]

References
1. F J Furnivall, cited in C E Raven, *Christian Socialism 1848-1854*, London, 1920, 1968 edn, p 55.
2. Stanley G Evans, *The Social Hope of the Christian Church*, Hodder, 1965, p 153.
3. W Rauschenbusch, *Christianising the Social Order*, 1912, p 124.
4. K S Inglis, *Churches and the Working Classes in Victorian England*, 1963, p 251.
5. *Church Reformer* X: 10, October 1891, p 124.
6. Frederick Verinder, 'The Bible and the Land Question', *Church Reformer*, vol IV, 7, 15 July 1885.
7. *Ibid*, V, 7, p 146.
8. M B Reckitt, *P E T Widdrington: A Study in Vocation and Versatility*, SPCK, 1961, p 3.
9. Lewis Donaldson, 'Church and Socialism Face to Face', *The Church Socialist*, October, 1913, p 4.
10. *COPEC Commission Reports*, Longmans, 1924, Vol 1, p 98.
11. D L Munby, *God and the Rich Society*, 1961, p 158.
12. *Magnificat*, 20 May 1944.
13. *Catholic Crusader*, 16 January 1933, p 3.
14. *Manifesto*, Notes, 20.
15. *Catholic Crusader*, 23, 16 January 1933, p 6.
16. *Russia Reviewed*, Religion and the People Publications, 1956, p 9.
17. *Manifesto*, Introduction, p 7.
A fuller list of references for this article may be obtained from the author.

9. From Temple to *Slant* (Aspects of English Theology 1945-1970)*

John Kent

William Temple's *The Church Looks Forward* (1944) makes a convenient starting-point. There Temple, looking to the post-war situation, advocated as the ideal an integrated society on a coherent Christian pattern. He argued that 'the Church' — for him essentially the Church of England — had the right to lay down the principles which should govern the ordering of human society 'because in the revelation entrusted to it, it has an understanding of man and his destiny dependent upon that revelation, which illuminates every phase of human conduct'.[1]

This position appealed to a conservative theological tradition which claimed that the right understanding of human nature and therefore of politics depended upon an acceptance of the Christian revelation as a body of knowledge mediated by the Church as a supernatural body. This system of knowledge included the doctrine of original sin, which had to be taken as a fact however mythological its expression, and might be taught in schools, public and private, as the key to the understanding of human history. In the years after 1945 belief in the possibility of a single, theologically integrated society waned steadily but the idea that their knowledge of original sin gave theologians an advantage over humanists and Marxists remained firm. Sinful men needed to be redeemed, and therefore in Temple's view there could be 'no hope of establishing a more Christian social order except through the labour and sacrifice of those in whom the Spirit of Christ is active'.[2] Temple himself used the phrase 'original sin' to mean not only that each human personality was initially imperfect, but that the necessary reorganisation of the self required the assistance of divine grace. The kind of political comment which grew from this root and which dominated much of the theology of the 1950s as a

* A version of this paper was given at a meeting of the Christendom Trust at Sussex University in July 1976, and first published in *The Epworth Review*, vol 4, no 1, January 1977.

kind of new pessimism may be seen in this passage from V A Demant's
Theology and Society (1947):

> 'The believer who has won some insight into the meaning of original
> sin and the need of grace knows that also the extent of what is wrong
> in organised society is out of all proportion to the deliberately anti-
> social or defective behaviour of persons and groups in it at any one
> time. He knows the corrupting effects of the collective miasma of
> sinfulness upon the best intentions, the good motives and the altruistic
> actions of personal and corporate wills ... the first question which the
> Christian mind will ask of a social order is whether its organisation
> recognises the moral frailty of man.'[3]

Thirty years later, E R Norman wrote of a fundamental division or tension
in the relationship of Christianity to the world: 'a dialectic between that
attitude which would seek to regenerate men individually to render them
fit to change society; and that which, on the contrary, would first change
society by immediate political means in order to create the conditions
necessary for educating men into regeneration'.[4] Both themes were
evident in Temple and recurred in his successors. He said, for example, in
1944, that 'the purpose of God is quite plainly something that can be
described in the formula "the development of persons in community" '.[5]
At the same time, from the 1941 Malvern Conference until his death,
Temple was trying to form what he termed 'a body of influence guided by
Christian principles'[6] to plead in the post-war period for proper housing
for all; adequate nutritional standards for all; and education up to
eighteen for all as far as this was practicable. These detailed proposals
related less to the dogma of original sin than to his conviction that the
divine purpose in human society could be grasped and identified as 'the
supremacy in all respects of the human person'.[7] The gap between the
programme and the ideal was perhaps a comment on the lopsidedness of
British society. Temple was less impressive in his refusal to initiate
disestablishment: 'we have a divine commission; we exist as a divine
creation. If the earthly state likes to associate itself with us, let it. If it
would rather separate itself off, let it. But our business is to be true to the
commission we have received: to proclaim unchanged the unchanging
gospel of God.'[8] The glossy phrases concealed politics, not theology:
establishment required two parties and, whatever divine commission the
Church of England might have as a spiritual body, it had no absolute
divine commission to be established. The statement that the Church of
England leaders would retain the possibilities and privileges of
establishment as long as the state did not take them away was honest, was
politically astute, at any rate in the short run, but was hardly a shining

example of Christian principle. As for 'the unchanging gospel of God', this was sheer magniloquence.

If one then asks, what happened to Christian political thought in the post-war period, one answer would be to turn to an essay by David Jenkins, 'The Concept of the Human', included in a volume edited by R H Preston, *Technology and Social Justice* (1971). Jenkins quoted a sentence from the third section of the WCC Uppsala Report — 'the central issue in development is the criteria of the human'.[9] The obvious link with Temple was that his programme of the 1940s had been expressed in the slogan, 'the supremacy in all respects of the human person' (see above). Jenkins himself did not propose a political programme, even of the limited kind which Temple had drawn up (housing, nutrition, education), but he suggested that the concept of the human held by a Christian depended upon the prior belief that a living God had created the world and was to be known 'immanently in the core of our own being'.[10] This meant (he said) that the resources of grace were available in any situation; what mattered in a given political problem was 'the struggle of faith to bridge the gap between the observable and experienced realities ... and the glimpsed possibilities which have been seen in the gospel'.[11] If one asked what values followed from this perspective, Jenkins replied that men must be treated as ends, not as means, a not unfamiliar quotation since the Enlightenment, but not from a specifically Christian source. It was a measure of the difference between Temple's over-confidence that the Church of England could still mount a political movement to influence post-war society, and Jenkins' experiences in Geneva at the WCC headquarters, that the latter asked 'whether entertaining concepts of the human makes any difference to the human situation — and this implies facing the question *how* a difference is made'.[12] Whereas Temple had had no doubt that one made a difference by holding public meetings, by forming local branches, by writing and distributing tracts, by working out a programme, in short, by organisation in the 19th century manner which had been perfected by Jabez Bunting, William Wilberforce and the Tractarians, Jenkins, having asked *how* this difference was to be made, answered that 'it seems to me extremely likely that there can be no definitive answer'.[13] At least one reason for Jenkins' despair, his recognition that an appeal to the 'criteria of the human' no longer meant turning to a settled 'liberal' consensus, was that the polarisation of modern international and domestic politics between Marxist and non-Marxist groups made it even more difficult than it had been in Temple's day to find a political programme which would not divide the religious institutions themselves. (Sex gradually replaced alcohol as the safe subject.) And the failure of the ecumenical movement deprived Temple's successors of what he had regarded as a great potential source of influence.[14]

In Jenkins' essay, therefore, one may detect the survival of Temple's belief in Christian principles and in the central importance of human personality, as well as traces of a sophisticated political scepticism. The world had changed so much since 1945, and the religious institutions of the West had had little to do with causing the changes. China, for instance, had been unified and partially transformed on a neo-Marxist basis; similarly, Burma, India, Pakistan and Indonesia had been freed from the control of Western and Christian cultural forces; Islam had revived, in faith as well as on oil; Africa had become far more rapidly independent than seemed possible during the second world war. The United States of America, at once the arsenal of Western politics and the proof that Western religious institutions could expand in the twentieth century, had committed a dreadful kind of spiritual suicide all over Vietnam and become a liability to the Western religious tradition. In another quarter altogether, Judaism, for so long dismissed from history by Christian theologians, had re-entered time once and for all through the oven-door of the 'final solution', and had become yet again the inner question-mark of the European and Christian tradition. And the swift decline of Britain altered with each decade, so that by the late 1970s the formerly united kingdom faced the probability of political disintegration. For this last, domestic conflict, the return of the celtic twilight, religious institutions bore more obvious responsibility. To an Englishman not unaware of the problems of Northern Ireland (and Eire for that matter) it seemed incredible that the WCC should have met in Africa in 1976 under the shadow of the claim that 'Jesus Christ frees and unites'.

One has the impression that Christian political thought in England marked time after 1945 until the publication of *Honest to God* (1963) introduced a period of theological confusion which was reflected in this as in other areas. It was obvious in the post-war years that religious institutions were not powerful enough, or even influential enough, to make the state pay attention to the allegedly Christian principles which were laid down by such bodies as the Lambeth Conference and the Methodist Conference as freely as ever. The Anglican report on divorce, with its ignominious title, *Putting Asunder* (1964-66), which preceded changes in the divorce law (1969) which substituted the concept of 'marriage breakdown' for the older 'matrimonial offence', was good evidence of the way the tide was really flowing. (And if one is discussing political theology it is not enough to talk about what might happen in the future, one has to go back to the way in which things are happening.) The Anglican Committee repeated that *for Anglicans* the marriage contract was permanent, and that therefore a secular decree of divorce did not entitle either party to remarry within the rites of the Church, a position reaffirmed, after much argument, in 1974, but accepted the idea of 'breakdown', which came from lawyers (not theologians) who had tired of the humbug of the previous system, as the basis of the new secular law. The Committee comforted itself with a superb example of verbal politics:

'We further believe that the principle of breakdown might make secular divorce in some respects less offensive to Christian sentiment than it is now. Under the existing law the impression left is that the State is arrogating to itself a power which, according at least to the Western tradition inherited by the Church of England, is not given to man, namely, the power to dissolve valid consummated marriage, and to put asunder what (so Christians believe) God has made one. It is true, as we have noted, that all the State in fact claims is authority to cancel the legal rights and duties associated with marriage, since it does not take cognisance of any more deeply seated vinculum. Nevertheless under the existing system the unpleasant impression is hard to exorcise. Under a system based on breakdown, however, what the divorce court appeared to be doing might be less disturbing. It would no longer seem to say to a petitioner, "We authorise you to put away your partner because he or she has committed such and such an offence"; rather it would seem to say, "We find on enquiry that this marriage relationship has so irretrievably disintegrated that it is no longer qualified to receive legal recognition: therefore legal recognition is withdrawn." That surely would be a gain.'[15]

This flight into fiction, in which the state 'would no longer seem to say' what (according to one version of the Christian rules for marriage) it *ought* not to say, may enable us to see more closely how this post-war period illustrated the problem of Christian praxis. Politically, the superficial problem was that as long as Anglican theorists felt that the Church of England was, however arguably, the religious expression of the 'national culture' — and they were still maintaining this in the 1970 Chadwick report on Church and State, however pungently Miss Valerie Pitt might dissent in an appendix — they were also bound to feel that the 'Anglican' principle of the indissolubility of marriage ought, however inoperatively, to be the 'national' principle as well. Theoretically, this committed the leaders of the Church of England to political action about marriage and divorce in a sense in which the Roman Catholic leaders, though sharing the position in principle, were not committed. Serious *political,* as distinct from *prophetic,* action, however, if it is to be of any magnitude, requires a basis in the living conditions and feelings and wishes of a sizeable section of the population, and after 1945 neither the Anglican nor the Roman Catholic leadership could stimulate sizeable lay resistance to an easing of the state divorce laws. This might be a matter of principle but it was not a political issue.

Of course, the Lambeth Committee produced an exposition of Genesis which justified the change in principle, but ingenuity of that kind only diminished the authority of the appeal to the Bible. The change was so clearly a yielding to social pressures (it is true that the Roman authorities remained unmoved by Lambeth's use of Genesis, but behind the scenes few people denied that it was the psychological cost of yielding, not the practical effect of resisting, which was really decisive) that theology was bound to be affected. Was there an immutable, revealed deposit of knowledge which theology applied to society in time; or was there no body of Christian principles available after all? David Jenkins might still be asking the 'how' question in 1971, but others were wondering what 'concepts of the human' could be trusted as Christian. Did one invoke the spirit of the age and the spirit of Christ in one fearful alchemy? And would they come if we did call to them?

At this stage some sort of dialogue with Marxism became inevitable even against the English background. The best example is the short-lived *Slant* movement of younger Catholics in 1966. The leader was perhaps Terry Eagleton, 23 at the time, about to become Oxford's tame Marxist literary critic and to publish books on Victorian novelists. His book, *The New Left Church* (1966), was a bundle of loosely linked essays, some of them more about literature than politics, but this, and the *Slant Manifesto* (1966), edited by Neil Middleton, were the principal documents of one of the contributory streams which fused, farcically (as I would say), in 1968. Eagleton, perhaps because he was Catholic and not Anglican, had grasped that the line of thought and action which had passed from William Temple down to Jenkins and others was not going to produce radical change. (Neither was the alternative he was proposing, but that was not yet obvious to him in 1965-66.) He said that 'most real social action' and Christian reformism in general 'is blocked or qualified by a fundamental commitment to the status quo'.[16] He combined this kind of statement:

'Since the resurrection, the meaning of human community has been Christ. Whenever two or three are gathered together, in a pub or discussion group or works committee, Christ is the ground of their communication, the living principle of their community,'[17]

with this more evidently political reference:

'The idea that the experience of the worker under capitalism is one of alienation is one of Marx's most basic insights, and forms the centre of Marxist humanism.'[18]

He had clearly not read T W Adorno's *The Jargon of Authenticity* (1964)
– the Frankfurt Marxist school's critique of Kierkegaard, Heidegger and
Tillich; so he could write:

> 'We have said that to live authentically is to live the life of human
> community and therefore the life of Christ. To make an authentic act
> of personal self-affirmation is thus to affirm the human community
> and Christ: to be most purely oneself is to point beyond oneself.'[19]

The solution which probably owed more to Raymond Williams than to
Frankfurt, he summed up in this way:

> 'The radical response to an alienated society is the response of
> community – community as the way of life in which all men can be
> simultaneously free subjects, present to each other without mutual
> exploitation ... For the Christian there is a prototypal society in which
> this can happen, and this is the liturgy. In the eucharist the individual
> "projects" of each member are resolved and reconciled in Christ:
> Christ is the living unity which resides in the interior of each
> subjectivity, the whole community present simultaneously within each
> member of it ... We need to build a political society where the unity
> of the whole community can be interiorised within each member of
> it.'[20]

As to method, he remained significantly uncommitted:

> 'We have to decide whether we are the kind of radical who is prepared
> to use almost any weapon to bring about justice, or whether we
> believe that the way that justice comes is part of its meaning: if this is
> our position, we have to ask ourselves whether, in believing that we can
> establish a Christian society without dirtying our hands, we are merely
> making a stock liberal underestimation of what it will take to build
> that society.'[21]

The *Slant* episode ended quickly, partly because the Catholic hierarchy in
England reacted smoothly, encouraging discussion, and burying the
political issue under gentle requests for a detailed programme of action;
partly because Raymond Williams himself, writing in *New Blackfriars,*
dismissed the proposed combination of Catholicism and the New Left as
superfluous: Marxism was complete in itself, did not need religious
metaphors. There was to be no equivalent of the Garaudy episode in
England.[22]

It is tempting to analyse what happened in more detail. Part of

Eagleton's experience had been that of the Catholic sub-culture, a world still largely shut off from Protestant England by the walls of a separate consciousness, so that one inevitably thought of society as somewhere outside the 'church', a foreign territory to be invaded and transformed by aggressive Christians, or perhaps better avoided by pious Catholics. This Catholic sub-culture, like the Free Church sub-cultures to which it was related, was breaking up. The young men wanted an ecclesiology which would free them from their Victorian ecclesia; they wanted a political theology instead of pietism. They were not satisfied with the kind of role which they could play in the religious sub-cultures, but they were still so far captive to them that they needed to relate the religious language in which they had been trained to the new roles which they sought in the mainstream, predominantly secular culture. This explains the strange concoction of an existentialist ecclesiology and a Marxist political analysis, a formula to cover the break-out from the Old Jerusalem. The deeper reason for the collapse of *Slant,* and of the student mood of 1968, lay in the same area: the thirst for social significance and mobility, which was the content of that alleged revolutionary enthusiasm, could be satisfied within the existing socio-political system, leaving the revolutionaries free to fall back on various kinds of nostalgia when they felt themselves to have compromised. There was no 'peasant' discontent for the religious Marxists to harness – the 'peasants' had sensibly emigrated in the nineteenth century; the only people who still 'revolutionised' in terms of land were a tiny regressive section of the middle-class, who wanted land, but hid the craving in the creed of the religio-personalist commune. As for the car-workers, it was known that they must be alienated, but the Catholic Marxists imposed their own pattern on that, just as William Temple would have done.

So much for the 'political theology' of the past 30 years: what can one say that is relevant to the present? The following observations may be of interest:

1. A religious sub-culture still exists, though it resists attempts to give it coherence.

2. This sub-culture should not simply be described as middle-class. It is true that suburban congregations are overwhelmingly middle-class if one judges in terms of occupation, but there are congregations on working-class housing estates which draw from the clerical workers, the skilled manual workers and foremen and other non-manual workers, though there are few representatives of the 'partly skilled' and 'unskilled' occupations. The numbers involved in these latter congregations are small, however.

3. At least three levels of religious political activity follow: the institutional, including the British Council of Churches; the pressure-

groups (Mrs Whitehouse, for example); and local 'community-type' action.

4. Given the institutional structures and the clerical control of Anglicanism, Catholicism and Methodism, etc, it is inevitable that the whole sub-culture should reflect middle-class interests — peace, materialism, moral education, censorship. The period since 1945 suggests that institutional religious political action achieves little or nothing — the characteristic move is the retreat, as over divorce and contraception. The alternative mode of action is the religious political party, but the record of Christian Democratic parties in Europe suggests that one should not encourage the formation of a branch party in England. The introduction of proportional representation would make this a live option, and the clergy of an ecumenical church might well be enthusiastic.

5. Over the years 1945-1975 there was a slight increase of interest in revolution as a religious option. This is not surprising in England, which has become a boring country to live in, without a single novelist, poet, musician or painter of more than second-class ability; there are ominous overtones of a Weimar without the genius. If one assumes, for the sake of argument, that political Marxism is bound to predominate globally by the end of the next 30 years, one can envisage a scenario in which Europe turns communist politically in order to protect itself against the world outside. Then the religious sub-culture will need a strategy for coping with a radically new culture. Indeed, adjustment is what would be needed, not the hegelian long-haul; history is not essentially continuous and cannot be interpreted reliably by either hegelian or eschatological analysis. But it is time to end the favourite English middle-class game, no doubt a substitute for the lost empire, of vicarious imperialism, which is reflected at the religious institutional and pressure-group levels as an obsession with pseudo-action in South Africa or South America — any place which is a long way from the Welsh mining valleys or the quiet hells of outer London. It is time that the English came home imaginatively and set about that transformation of their own society, which they have put off for 100 years while they interfered with the societies of other races.

References

1. W. Temple, *The Church Looks Forward,* 1944, p 105.
2. *Ibid,* p 107.
3. V A Demant, *Theology and Society,* 1947, p 168.
4. E R Norman, *Church and Society in England,* 1976, p 14.
5. Temple, *op cit,* p 131.
6. *Ibid,* p 122.
7. *Ibid,* p 123.
8. *Ibid,* p 124.
9. D Jenkins, 'The Concept of the Human', in R H Preston (ed) *Technology and Social Justice,* 1971, p 205.

10. *Ibid,* p 221.
11. *Ibid,* p 224.
12. *Ibid,* p 217.
13. *Ibid,* p 217.
14. For Temple, see J F Padgett, *The Christian Philosophy of William Temple,* The Hague, 1974.
15. *Putting Asunder,* 1966, p 61.
16. T Eagleton, *The New Left Church,* 1966, p 86.
17. *Ibid,* p 142.
18. *Ibid,* p 158.
19. *Ibid,* p 169.
20. *Ibid,* p 166.
21. *Ibid,* p 179.
22. R Garaudy left the French Communist Party on the religious issue.

PERSPECTIVES

10. Agenda for Prophets - Religion and What?

Stephen Yeo

'*Let every Christian as much as in him lies engage himself openly and publicly before all the World in some Mental pursuit for the Building up of Jerusalem,*' William Blake, in *Jerusalem,* chap 4.

'*The prophets of old ... addressed themselves to those who thought they did God's service and did it not. We address ourselves to those who do God's service and know it not,*' John Trevor (of the Labour Church Movement) in *Seedtime* (1896).

This chapter[1] is addressed to and comes from a sense of inadequacy. If, as a generation of social thinkers in Britain (let alone as a generation of Christian social thinkers), we do not rate very highly, this is not entirely our fault. Christian social thought has been a victim along with many other kinds of ambitious, systematic social thought and action, of the weight of 'consensus' about 'the end of ideology' (theology), 'piecemeal social engineering', and so on. Christian organisations have also been the victims, along with many other organisations, of overwhelming contextual pressures towards privatised, 'apathetic' consumer capitalism. The period from about 1948 until about 1968 in Britain was a period of extreme difficulty, not just for Christian prophecy (unless of eccentric kinds) but for radical secular vision as well.[2] Nor is this a simple matter of context *and* organisations or ideas: rather is it a matter of organisations or ideas *in* context, which they themselves compose in a continual process of action and reaction. In all our work we have to be conscious of a complicating double optic. We have to see how much we are part of the problem before we can be part of the solution.

Now, however, such weights against prophecy are losing their gravity. 'Crisis' has begun to acquire a resonance within metropolitan capitalisms like our own and outside a few eccentric circles, secular or otherwise. New opportunities, as well as ever-escalating costs of failure, present themselves. And Christianity, after all, offers a timelessness and a placelessness of perspective which can rescue us from the common sense of our own times and places. It encourages us to dare to think that things are not what they seem: to attempt to see the whole in order to see the parts. It offers powerful levers for systematic understanding which secular powers are bound to discourage us from pulling.

Having said that, this chapter will not prophesy. I share R H Tawney's quest for an answer to the question, 'Religion and ... what?' I also share his sense of incompetence, his conviction of his own inadequacy for answering that question for his own times.[3] It was not easy, but it became possible thanks to his work to answer it for the earlier period covered by *Religion and the Rise of Capitalism* (1926). What is our equivalent to '... and the Rise of Capitalism'?[4] We need, collectively, to know, or rather to make, an equivalent. Here I will merely suggest some materials towards doing so, some signs of the times a prophet today would have to interpret unless she or he fancied the wilderness.

There are, first, the changing forms of capitalist organisation in our society – in production and distribution most fundamentally – but particularly during the twentieth century in branches of production such as leisure, communications, and in aspects of life sometimes referred to as 'culture'.

Second, the altering presence of the State and centre, in relation to localities.

Third, the long crisis of class and democracy in Britain, particularly interesting in relation to other societies precisely because of its unique length. With this goes a manifest contradiction in our society between promise and performance.

Each of these summary headings bears on the huge question of the relationship between Christian understandings of humanity, association and God on the one hand, and *'religious'* organisations on the other. What is the place and nature of religious organisations (like our own churches and chapels) in the changing situation of voluntary associations as a whole?[5] They also bear on the critical, and related, problem of *agency*. For those who believe in an equal and self-governing society there is much uncertainty at the moment (Christian and otherwise) about precisely through what set of agencies such a society can be brought nearer to realisation. What do Christians have to say, not so much about goals as about *forms* of struggle? Can they get below the level of vague discussion of 'violence'?

The safety of an itemised agenda will leave these matters as questions, staying for an answer. I will take my three headings in turn.

I.

My text, as they say, is taken from *The British Weekly: A Journal of Christian and Social Progress.* On 24 September 1891 there appeared in that journal a letter from a 'Constant Reader', under the heading 'Pulpit Notices or the Latest Advertising Medium'.

'Sir,' it began,

'I take the liberty of addressing you on the matter of "Pulpit Notices" and to ask if something cannot be done to reform our present practice in the matter. I am sure many of my fellow-worshippers would rejoice if some other means were found of making known matters in connection with modern church work but which savour so much of the theatre and show that, whatever their aim, do most certainly succeed in interrupting that divine Sabbath peace which ought to pervade our time of worship. I have heard notices from the pulpit concerning bazaars, concerts, living wax-works, gymnasium performances etc., but I think last Sunday's experience capped all previous. In a suburban church, under the supervision of a young and promising pastor, after some ordinary notices as to a coming bazaar, the following appeal was made:

"In connection with this bazaar a well-known firm of coal merchants have promised us that if all our friends here will combine to buy all their coals of them, they will then, in proportion to the quantity of coals purchased, do so-and-so for us. Now, this is a well-known firm and I am sure you will get as good coals of them as anyone else, so if our friends will kindly take this up and get their coals in this way, we shall get the benefit according to the quantity, but to do this you must order all coals of our friend Mr .... whose address is ...."

'Need I say more? What a fine scope it opens up for "Pears Soap" and "Colmans Mustard"; but is it not time we drew the line somewhere?

'I am sir –

'Constant Reader'

Such deep involvement in dominant ways of distributing commodities has not been uncommon since the second half of the nineteenth century among a wide range of voluntary associations. Subordination has not always been so direct as it was to the 'well-known firm of coal merchants'. More commonly it has been a matter of language, or style, of imitation of business organisational methods and market assumptions, rather than of

direct take-over.[6] Late nineteenth century denominations with a working-
class constituency, such as the Primitive Methodists or the Salvation
Army, were explicitly turning to business modes as a way of protecting or
enabling mass growth. And religious organisations more generally were
actively dividing their potential clients into age-specific, gender-specific
and class-specific targets, and elaborating the divisions into clusters of sub-
agencies. What political scientists would call 'goal displacement' – doing
X in order to do Y and then finding oneself doing X *instead* of Y – was
becoming a galloping disease, causing great distress to serious ministers who
were 'successful' at it. 'Constant Reader' was not alone in identifying
these phenomena either: they were intermittently analysed and deplored
elsewhere in the late nineteenth century denominational press.

　'Is it not time we drew the line somewhere?' There is plenty of evidence
from the West coast of America, a frontier of religious innovation in the
1970s, that the line has by now been rubbed out amongst some Christians.
Salvation has become a commodity to be marketed like any other, and
denominations have become businesses to show a return like any other. A
utilitarian language of cost-effectiveness has penetrated our own Christian
discourses too. The problem has become how, not where, to draw the line.

　In tackling this question my assumptions are as follows: first, that
capitalism may be separated (to varying degrees in different periods) from
society, although at a certain date in the history of specific capitalisms it
becomes accurate to talk of a 'capitalist society'. In other words, different
modes of production coexist historically and encroach upon one another
over time.[7] Second, that we cannot get very far with the label 'capitalism'.
Not only does capitalism vary in extent within any single society, it also
varies in intensity. It has to be broken down into periods or phases of
development. Marx mapped its general nature, in work like Volume I of
Capital. It is less commonly realised how much he also drew the contours
in the same work by careful periodisation, notably with definitions of
'large-scale industry' over against manufacture and handicraft phases.
Third, that it is only relatively recently that areas of life such as leisure,
communications or even politics have become adequately, or
predominantly, capitalist. And it is still controversial how much such areas
of life should be understood as separate instances, separate that is to say
from 'economics' or material production narrowly understood. But 'mass'
leisure and 'mass' communication, connected as they are, have become
sectors of the economy crucial to its performance. We can look at them
and other areas of cultural production in ways similar to the ways we look
at more obviously 'economic' activities. As Christians, we have not really
recognised the importance of the changes since, as a Primitive Methodist
preacher observed in Reading early in the twentieth century, 'Abraham
could travel as fast as my grandfather'.

Fourth, that capitalism is defined by and depends upon specific antagonisms or *contradictions* — the central one being the capital-labour social relation. Such an assertion would need backing up to become acceptable or meaningful to most readers of this book. There is no space for this here: the only importance of the observation in this context is that, if correct, it builds *possibility* and *struggle* into the system as well as the functionalist *closure* which many Marxists (as well as others) succeed in effecting. Capitalism depends for its survival and growth on bringing into being the possibility of its overthrow: it cannot develop in straight lines, or realise the highest potential it creates and therefore has to contain. Illustration of this point later in this chapter may make it clearer.

My fifth assumption is that Christianity has a crucial stake in understanding the four assumptions above. Whether or not such a religion and its organisations understand and interpret such points, they are bound to be deeply affected by the social realities to which they refer. Consider, for instance, the pulpit. What is said in pulpits is one thing and is, of course, an important preoccupation for Christian social thought. But the salience of what is said, as well as the sermons themselves, cannot be understood without a range of contextual analysis, including the relations (antagonistic or otherwise) between the audience and those not present, and dominant technologies and forms of production and communication elsewhere in the culture. The Press and the Platform, as Silvester Horne understood, are only two of the contextual factors affecting the Pulpit.[8] In their classic work on *Middletown* (1929), H and M Lynd were very sensitive to the range of interdependent factors which had to be brought into play before an activity like preaching or church-going could be understood.[9] My point here is that the *preacher,* and not just the professional sociologist, has a necessary stake in detailing and interpreting such factors.

The argument which I would want to base upon these assumptions can be stated baldly, but is not simple. The argument is *not* that we should deplore the encroachment of capitalism on hitherto relatively unsocialised areas in the manner of a nineteenth century idealist prophet like Carlyle. Manifestations of capitalism (like *The Sun* newspaper) are only 'wrong' to the extent that capitalist modes themselves (like the organisation of the cotton industry) are wrong. Incidentally also, peoples' tastes, capacities, demands 'from below', can no more be deduced from the nature of manifestations of capitalism (like *The Sun* newspaper) than they can from capitalist modes themselves (like the organisation of the cotton industry). These are matters to be understood mainly but not exclusively in terms of patterns of supply from above and in terms of each other. *The Sun* newspaper cannot be understood *without* understanding the organisation of the cotton industry, as well as the phases of development of the capitalist newspaper industry. Too much Christian would-be prophecy is spent deploring manifestations such as the television or page three of *The Sun* and moralising about them as if consumers were primarily responsible.

The argument is rather that we have to try to get behind results into processes and struggles. We have to try to understand the context within which we move and particularly the penetration of changing modes of capitalist organisation into social (and geographical) areas where they have been less present, or present in less dominant ways, or in different forms. We have to try to understand the necessary and positive features of that context, as well as the ones which most obviously threaten our own beliefs and organisations. We have to try to understand the specifically modern features of capitalist organisation and, a slightly different task, those features of modern organisation which are specifically capitalist. The size of characteristic contemporary enterprises, many of them bigger than many States; the scale of capital involved and the high proportion of investment in plant rather than in labour, indeed the constant pressure from capital to extrude labour; the subordination of labour to the machine and the development of mass production and continuous flow 'factories'; the ever more elaborate and minute division of labour, meaning that a phrase like 'we are all members one of another' is rapidly assuming a material, economic meaning, and on a world scale; the organised separation of mental from manual labour and the development of the 'new class' of scientific and supervisory workers who may or may not be open to understanding in classical class terms; the process of what has been called 'de-skilling', which has ramifications in politics, voluntary associations, child-rearing and many areas of culture other than material production — these developments, along with others, and other ways of putting the same things which Christians may prefer, are all necessary grist for any late twentieth century prophetic mill.[10] We have to try and understand the possibilities such developments open up, as well as the constraints they impose, before we decide, if we do so decide, to 'oppose' them, or to oppose only the forms they take currently but not the technologies themselves, or to withdraw from them, or to welcome them with open arms in order to sprinkle as much holy water on them as we are allowed.

The speed and scale of changes in *ideas* relevant to theology from the eighteenth century enlightenment onwards, and the problems this posed for Christians, has become a commonplace. The speed and scale of changes in modes of production and distribution and consequently-dominant associational forms and the problems these pose for Christians have been insufficiently recognised. The problem for Christian social thought usually represented as Marxism is not a problem at all; the problems are the social realities to which Marxists, among others, are addressing themselves, which they are trying to understand and to change.

II.

The second item on my agenda is an aspect of the first: the changing presence of the State and centre in relation to the life of localities.

A contemporary prophet would surely have to recognise the sheer scale of the increase of the twentieth century State. This is not just a phenomenon of 'totalitarianism' either. It became visible to the naked eye in a liberal capitalism like our own British variety with the total state take-over during the 10 years of world war in this century. The apparatus was partly dismantled after World War I but remained in place to a considerable extent after 1945.[11] These war years were years of 'national socialism' or 'state capitalism' introduced, in the contradictory ways of twentieth century politics, in order to make the world safe for their opposite.[12] The process has been a relentless one, seemingly unstoppable. United Kingdom Public Expenditure in 1913 was 13.5 per cent of GNP: in 1968 it was 52.1 per cent. Of this, 4.7 per cent of GNP went on 'Social Services' in 1913, 26 per cent in 1968.

We could find endless indices of increase. Interpreting such indices is the real problem. Christians have a responsibility to see through self-serving ideology masquerading as fact of the kind now evident in the discussion on public spending limits. 'Public spending' is currently being presented as a kind of bonus, awarded to us in return for increased production. It thus becomes subject to withdrawal once bad behaviour, like asking for wage increases to maintain standards of living, becomes widespread. In reality, such public spending has either had to be fought for by labour or else it exists because it is also essential for private capital that it should exist. It is not an extra, an award for good behaviour. It is a precondition of successful production in modern competitive conditions. No one yet maintains that mass elementary schooling is an optional extra, or mass policing for that matter, or that there is a queue of entrepreneurs waiting to provide such goods in an adequate form privately. And yet the fact that there has been massive *public* provision of these and other goods is one of the major elements in the context within which all our associations have to move. 'Voluntary action', as W H Beveridge began to chart in 1948-9, has been placed under tremendous strain.[13] In just the same way that it is difficult to start a car factory once the concentration of capital in that industry has gone very far, so too it has become difficult to undertake any ambitious cultural/social/political initiative except through 'the State' or one of its organs. 'More than ever before,' Ralph Miliband began his book *The State in Capitalist Society* (1969), 'men now live in the shadow of the State. What they want to achieve individually, or in groups, now mainly depends on the State's sanction or

support.' What is the specifically Christian response to such a situation?
Or are there as many Christian responses as there are people calling
themselves Christians?

The next thing that a contemporary prophet would have to recognise
would be the paradoxical irrelevance of this vastly-increased twentieth
century State in its *national* forms, or rather its subordination to other
centres of power, such as international companies, World Banks,
International Monetary Funds and the like. This is clear in relation to
nation-states which are smaller than the companies with 'outlets' within
their territories. But it is also obvious (at least to Chancellors of the
Exchequer) in metropolitan capitalisms. Nowadays planners can pull the
levers and the signals do not move, press the brakes and the train does not
slow down. The signal box and the engine driver seem to have moved,
although they occasionally summon us or honour us with a visit. What the
exact relation between private concentrations of capital, international
capitalist organisations and States now is, is a matter of active debate and
controversy. All I can say here, in line with my agenda-making rather than
prophetic role, is that Christians are well placed in this matter (they have
universal rather than national commitments and developed international
organisations well before anyone else), and that the contemporary
equivalent to the Liberal debate on the philosophy of the State to which
earlier Christian social thought can be related (T H Green, B Bosanquet,
H Belloc, L T Hobhouse, et al) is probably the debate on the nature of
the modern state between socialists such as R Miliband and N Poulantzas
in journals like the *New Left Review.* It is urgently necessary for us to
'catch up' with such thinking, not in order to be able to jump on it as a
bandwagon, but in order to have some meaningful views on the realities
to which the debate undoubtedly refers.

Next, there is the space for Christian prophecy left by the fact that, as
Maurice Reckitt and others observed at the time of Guild Socialism,
statism has to a considerable extent taken over socialism. It has long been
obvious how polluted the word 'Communism' has been by twentieth
century history. So much so that we can no longer use it in the proud
manner of William Morris. It has only recently become apparent how
polluted the word 'socialism' has also been. It is doubtful whether its
major developments during the twentieth century have been in the
interests of the working class: its lack of resonance among most British
workers today may be less odd than socialists are tempted to think.
Socialism has been captured by a 'new class' of social administrators and
experts. The space for Christian prophecy, or indeed for creative 'socialist'
thought in general, lies in the no-man's-land between the ravages of
National Socialism, Stalinism and social democracy. Social democracy has
become the ideology of statism. Leave it to us, we are the experts, we

know better than you what you need, we define 'the national interest', we are the planners, the rationalisers, the technocrats: the best things happen from above, not from below. This ideology has become essential for the continued existence of capitalism. Whether or not it is the Labour Party which does the job, an agency which comes to resemble it in practice (as, of course, Margaret Thatcher will have to do if she wishes to remain in office) is an essential prop for our present social order.

There is therefore something of a vacuum here for movement builders to occupy, in a way that there probably has not been since the early 1920s. The exciting thing is that there is competition for filling it. Neither Stalinism nor social democracy of the kind I am describing has ever been a popular *working-class* ideology. And I shall be referring below to other strands of radical, collective self-help which flourished particularly in the last half of the nineteenth century and which had to be driven underground and 'licensed' lest they burst out of their capitalist shell altogether during the twentieth century. But now there are some signs of creative social energy from below in trade unions and elsewhere, tapping these hidden streams. In community politics, feminism, new kinds of pressure groups resembling the 'moral reform crusades' of the first half of the nineteenth century, rank-and-file 'unofficial' movements at the points of production and elsewhere, there are signs of collective attempts at self-government all over again. It is in this space that Christian prophets will have to move.

III.

What do I mean by the third item on my agenda: the long crisis of democracy in Britain, and by the contradiction between promise and performance which is, to me, so manifest in our society?

So many crucial things have happened in Britain and so much *could* happen in Britain to fulfil and to transform some of those things... I come back and back to this reflection in what might look to be a naive chauvinist fashion, at a time when the insignificance in world terms of what is happening in Britain seems like common sense.

There have been obvious 'firsts', such as an early capitalist agriculture followed by industrial capitalism: Manchester and all that followed from it both in action and reaction – cotton, Free Trade *and* Engels/Marx – facts of epoch-making importance in nineteenth century world history and analyses of those facts which may or may not be capable of helping another epoch into being in twentieth and twenty-first century world history. There have been obvious exports and cultural inventions: not only empire, but a whole range of associations and activities from Methodism to Association Football, from the YMCA to Boy Scouts. Some of the exports have been destructive, including finished cotton which destroyed the Indian and Egyptian cotton industries. Some have been creative, or potentially so. Not the 'Parliamentary institutions' most frequently cited and least frequently imitated, but the constitutional forms, democratic devices, agitational styles, class movements, modes of self-organisation and struggle which were originally developed in the fight to wrest those Parliamentary institutions from a 'divine right' oligarchy during the seventeenth century, and which need to be developed further as part of the fight to wrest democracy from the ossified institutions and forms currently sitting upon it. We need the same energy and creativity concerning economic, social and political forms as our Reformation forebears exhibited in the 'religious' area.

There are now so many obvious 'lasts' that they amount to a crisis, no longer perceived as such only by secular socialist prophets. The senses in which Britain has become 'last' have been repeated inaccurately in hundreds of speeches and 'State of the Nation' messages, ever since Harold Wilson introduced the league table metaphor into our national self-consciousness in those pre-1964 days of the white heat of the technological revolution, the 13 wasted years, the 'Let's Go With Labour and We'll Get Things Done' sloganising. We are supposed to be growing more slowly, striking more often, innovating planning and managing less competently, investing less, demanding more impetuously, importing more, exporting less... than those in the same division of our international league. Or so we are told. Recently we have become an economy which suffers from being a 'low-wage' economy *and* from wage militancy! The connection between being first and being last is seldom pointed out, for to do so might provoke demands for being first again, in something quite new. This would involve dispossessing those currently profiting from our being last. The name of the disease changes quinquennially, from balance of payments deficits (needing 'rectifying'), to trade unionism (needing 'curbing'), to inflation (needing 'slowing down'), to public spending (needing 'cutting'). The medicine is the same: speeches, sticks, carrots, plus those 'budgetary measures' with which we have become familiar. Whatever the doctor says before he is called to the House, he has been watched by the patient altering the label on the same bottle so often that he is no longer called with any expectation of cure. Judging by election turnout, many citizens never call him at all.

In fact, to use a favourite Christendom phrase, we have been moralising a contradiction for far too long. There used to be a dominant moral interpretation of poverty which suggested that the poor were poor not because of low wages and competition, but because they drank too much, saved too little, beat their wives and lacked 'character'. The aim was to suggest a happy coincidence between moral worth and quantity of worldly goods possessed. This has now, broadly speaking, been jettisoned. But parallel moral interpretations of political alienation, economic crisis, or even of institutional religious decline, have grown up in its place.

In what then does the contradiction consist? To declare myself straight away, I believe that it inheres in the capital-labour social relation. But I also believe (against many modern Marxists) that the argument and empirical investigation *starts* rather than ends with such an assertion. There are at least three levels – (a), (b), (c) – on which the argument must now be carried forward.

(a) First, it is a necessary preliminary and possibly more than that, to show in detail the way in which the moralising is not just wrong but, because it is wrong, serves an important function in maintaining the position of those who employ it. In fact, to show that the moralising acts as an ideology, in the sense of a body of ideas serving to mask the realities of social relations. The moralising serves to prevent the contradictions being resolved in one way rather than another: more specifically, it serves to prevent the contradictions being resolved in the interests of those who do not own the means to produce the world's material and cultural goods rather than those who do. To develop this properly would mean following through one particular sub-category of the moralising, and to show its function in some detail.[14] The history and the material or class basis of dominant ways we have in our society of seeing each other as aggregates (eg as 'masses'), and the incompatibility of some of these ways of seeing with any Christian way or with theological understandings of Man, seems to me to be an important area for work.

There are more central sub-categories of moralisation than ones like 'apathy' or 'masses'. They relate more directly to economic, as opposed to social/political/cultural behaviour. It may be that dominant contemporary ways of seeing 'the British sickness' as a problem for moral reformation ('work harder', 'ask for less', 'give a pound for Britain', 'don't rock the boat', 'strengthen family life' – incidentally the depth of Christian attachment to our specific contemporary *family* patterns has long seemed to me to be a mystery of social/religious development needing unravelling and challenging in a very detailed way) are dominant because there is only one other way of seeing that sickness – namely to see it as a problem of over-readiness, of rotten-ripeness, of suppressed potential, of inhibited energy, towards a totally different social order.

Just as there is an ever-diminishing freedom of manoeuvre economically for British capitalism, so too there may be a diminishing freedom of manoeuvre ideologically. As the corner gets tighter and as the more accurate explanations of the sickness and the social movements behind them loom larger, we may expect increasingly shrill reaffirmations of the moralising explanation, which will offer the Church and its archbishops a seductive but essentially mystifying role. False prophets will arise, looking uncommonly like a cross between Edward Heath, Mary Whitehouse, Harold Wilson and Donald Coggan. They may even assume the more sinister shape of the Revd Moon of South Korea. Organised evangelism has been getting steadily more sinister since Billy Graham, Nixon's favourite Christian. The false prophets will have the odd entertainer from the glamour industry, the odd professional communicator from the newspaper industry, the odd ex-Prime Minister and the odd board member from that well-known would-be company Great Britain Limited (motto, democracy is inefficient) at their side. Most liberals and even the odd trade union leader will rally round. If exhortation does not work, 'sterner measures' will be applied. I will be dismissed as paranoid, but I am serious in saying that this is the soil from which a mutant of Fascism can grow, and can be supported by good Christians. After all, most Fascists in Germany were not always Fascists. Research increasingly shows that they were ordinary people, just like you and me, with unfulfilled needs. Many of them were Christians. Which is why alternative prophecy is so urgent now; naming and analysing the contradictions in the light of our understanding of what it is to be human in society in the light of our understanding of God's purposes, and daring to advocate the resolution of the contradictions on the side of righteousness, not at a millenial 'revolutionary' stroke but through a deliberately chosen process of struggle which, because we are Christians, prefigures the ends in the means. How can we trust each other as children of God and treat God as our Father in tangible social form? How, as E P Thompson asked in his essay, 'Outside the Whale' (1960), can love 'be expressed in human relations and embodied in history'? How can love become 'an effective and active social attitude' rather than only 'a personal resolution ... a state of personal experience'? There is not much time before the nuclear power industry either destroys us or forces us to freeze social relations as they are. We must indeed 'love one another or die'.

(b) The second level on which the argument could now be carried forward is less preliminary, more substantive. To demonstrate a contradiction between promise and performance means, I fully realise, to demonstrate the reality of the promise: to talk of suppressed potential means to show the reality of the potential: to talk of institutions and forms sitting on democracy rather than expressing it, means to demonstrate an impulse from below on which those institutions *could* be sitting. These demonstrations in turn involve a whole interpretation of modern British history and society which I can only sketch but which, I would suggest, a prophet might be interested in debating.[15]

This second level means pointing to the social forces behind one side of the contradiction: the social forces behind the other side (performance as opposed to promise) are, as I have pointed out, more familiar as part of the daily rhetoric of political debate, since about 1870 rather than only since the early Harold Wilson years. My brief answer to where these social forces are – namely in the working class and sometimes but crucially not always in the organised working-class movement – is likely to be misunderstood. I am *not* trying to remake the old equation between organised Labour and Christianity which P E T Widdrington and the Christendom Group had to break before they could start a new phase of prophecy after World War I.[16] But I will try to say what I mean.

Britain has long had a peculiarly powerful and peculiarly organised labour movement. This, according to the moralisers, is one of the problems: our position in the league table, they say, is not unconnected with the fact that about 36 per cent of trade unionists in Common Market countries and Britain in 1968 were trade unionists in Britain. And that these trade unionists are 'too powerful'. The British labour movement, for example miners' trade unions which included one in six of all trade unionists in Britain as late as 1920, has been extraordinarily creative from a democratic point of view. Internally and sectionally, and occasionally federally, it has managed to create mini-republics – communities of consciousness, interest and organisation (sometimes not unconnected with Christianity in various so-called 'primitive' forms) which twentieth century capital and the twentieth century state have found it necessary to destroy, because their demands were incompatible with the continued development of private capital in new conditions. The General Strike of 1926 was an episode in their destruction, which has never been unresisted and has never been complete. The fiftieth anniversary celebrations and historical work on the General Strike in many localities during 1976 were themselves testimony to the incompleteness of the destruction, as is the flourishing of labour and social history 'from below' during the last 20 years. This incompleteness is part of the political space within which we have now to move and which we have to try to understand as Christians.

Generalising the partial, preliminary achievements of 'labour aristocrats' during the period c1850-1900 to the whole class after 1900, would have meant a new social system, resembling and containing the potential for socialism or an associated mode of production, but not State socialism. The late nineteenth and early twentieth centuries may be seen partly as a long counter-attack on the culture, position and achievements of the organised labour movement over the previous 50 years, in which, ironically, social democracy and the Labour Party have played a major role. Indeed one might even say that this has been the historical mission of social democracy – to attenuate politics until 'politics' becomes mainly the secret, quinquennial ballot for most people and a job for a few. The formidable achievements of the self-activity of the working-class, or those sections of the class who had the time and the money, in building movements/organisations of world-historical importance such as Chartism, Co-operation, Friendly Societies and Trade Unions, are hard for us now to grasp – with our prepackaged ideology about 'mass apathy', and about how present social arrangements and present styles have come about because 'most people' wanted it that way. I cannot possibly evoke the warrening of capitalism which had gone on in Britain by 1900 here, but I would assert that it is crucial data for twentieth century Christian social perspectives. As one of their main tasks today prophets have to try to insert their wedges in the little cracks between demand and supply which an understanding of history can enable them to see, and then to drive the wedges home against the prevailing ideology which suggests an entire coincidence or perfect fit between demand and supply. What happens is not 'what most people really want' nor does it illustrate 'what most people are really like'. There is some space between what is and what could be, space for our historical, political and theological imaginations to get to work.

Only when the distance travelled in Britain, say by 1900, has been understood, can the journey since then also be understood. The impossibility of generalising the achievements, but not the demands, of the labour aristocrats to the rest of the class created a new situation demanding new thought, new modes of struggle appropriate to genuine mass politics. In the same way, the impossibility of continuing to compete in the world market with outmoded means and relations of production created a new situation demanding new modes of production and industrial organisation appropriate to genuine mass or associated production, 'social production controlled by social foresight'.

The subsequent situation of deadlock, with neither side able to push its own imperatives successfully through, is what I mean by the long crisis of class and democracy in Britain. The successor to liberal capitalism has not been fully born: there is still time, although it is running out fast, to help to influence whether it will be 'apathetic', corporatist, elitist, authoritarian, dehumanised international monopoly capitalism in Britain (as seems 95 per cent certain) or whether it can be as new a form of working-class democracy as Britain's industrial revolution was for its time and (middle) class. The impasse has long been apparent. Outlines of the crisis of democratic form were sketched in pioneering ways by the Webbs, Lenin, Michels, Schumpeter and others earlier in the twentieth century. Outlines of answers were put forward. But the extent to which there was inadequate or no follow-through, and the tiny role played by Christians both in discerning the problem and in sketching and evaluating answers, has been striking. How can one resist the main abortions of twentieth century universalising democracy, such as Stalinism or Fascism? Is democracy of the 'classical' kind hopeless in modern conditions? The twentieth century answer in societies like our own has been to take up arms (courageously and successfully) against 'the enemies of democracy' (eg 1939-45) and then lay them down with a sigh, complaining that the fighting started because people were too dissatisfied with what they had, and therefore overheated political systems by making too many demands on them.

What answers other than these disillusioned and unambitious sighs against the enemies of an open society can *we* give? The fact that there have not been many good Christian answers has provided the space within which heresies such as Moral Rearmament, Scientology or Jehovah's Witnesses have been able to flourish, on soil parched for want of alternative prophecy. Are there forms of democracy (localised, federated, uniting production with self-government, frequently meeting and debating as the occasions arise but then disciplined in executing, delegatory...) specifically suitable to a movement or society run by and in the interests of the working class and thus abolishing class altogether: as opposed to forms of democracy (centralised, based upon rigid divisions of labour and function, routinised on a set time-table like the Parliamentary calendar, based upon consumer modes such as the annual or quinquennial local or national vote in a private booth, representative) specifically suitable to a society run by and in the interests of the middle class? It was seventeenth century protestants who put such questions on the agenda, can we take them up? Can we let our answers to such questions be part of our Christian beliefs?

Are there ways of uniting the struggle for new forms with the new forms themselves, in such a way as not to make the characteristic twentieth century 'revolutionary' (Leninist) severance between means and ends? If there is a sense in which, since about the 1920s, the organised labour movement has been incorporated, and socialism has become statism, then how do we interpret a characteristic twentieth century working-class reaction to this phenomenon, namely to vote with the feet, or go fishing? Do we not have to discover the ways in which absolute powerlessness corrupts, just as our predecessors did with absolute power? What are the meanings of privatisation (another aspect of 'apathy'), other than its convenience for the consumption of commodities? What is the meaning to participants of fishing, gardening, do-it-yourself: or of conversation about football or the weather? What can they tell us about the surrounding social order and people's attitudes to it? Are they indicators of happy sheep looking up and being fed? Or of a flock who know what they are being offered, know at the moment that they do not like it and cannot much influence it, feed on the attenuated areas of green grass left uncontaminated but, at the right time and given the right circumstances, may be ready to choose shepherds and break out from private pastures into common fields? What is the role of Christian theology and Christian organisation in all this? Blessing, legitimising, propping up the repressive forces? Or daring to play the role of speculative, exploratory shepherds? It is all very well to ask questions. I fully realise that to answer any one of them properly might mean years of work. But we might as well start.

(c) The third level on which the argument could now be carried forward is the most difficult. I do not claim to be an adequate economist, let alone an adequate Marxist theoretician. Nor do I suggest that within Marx*ism,* particularly when it is seen as doctrine rather than as method, all the answers or all the questions are to be found. But I do wish to reclaim economics from economists, and suggest that the 'science' is too important in all our lives to be left to economists, Marxist or otherwise. Deference in this context is not a Christian virtue. R H Tawney spent much of his passion trying to understand, as a preliminary to being able to reverse, the historical process through which toadying had come to be regarded by Christians as virtuous and by capitalists as convenient. We should show our respects to Tawney by trying to continue, which does not mean to imitate, his work. How? All I can do here is to assert some do's and don't's.

My original question in this section was, 'In what then does the contradiction consist?'. Sections (a) and (b) above have been notes towards an answer. The short answer is simple, although it can be put in many ways. The contradiction is between vision and actuality. Some of the other ways of putting it are: between historical tendency and present conjuncture, between latent demand and manifest supply, between need and surplus value, between class forces whose characteristic development lies in private ownership, profit, the wage relationship, exploitation and competition-tending-towards monopoly, and class forces whose characteristic development lies in as yet undisclosed forms (although outlines can be sketched), but whose development certainly cannot proceed along the fullest human, understood in a Christian as well as a secular sense, lines while the class forces which *are* fully disclosed predominate.

Once I add these other ways of putting it, I suspect that the question for many Christian readers becomes, 'what has this got to do with vision and actuality?'. Stalinism and cold-war versions of Marxism have left the misleading impression that it is a finished science or doctrine; mainly about class battalions operating like 'determined' automata, manufacturing history regardless of will or morality. Instead, Marxism — in some of its contemporary versions — seems to me to offer a vision, and not for the first time either.[17] The vision is of an ending of the conflict between quantity and quality: a pulling down of politics (and of God) out of the sky and into human heads and hands – every human's hands, not the manicured few: a unity between all people and their products – the products being deliberately made through choice, distributed through need and real demand, and shared as things made by labour, not as things magic'd by money, mystified by price and multiplied for profit.

Only the best for all is good enough, and by being for all what is regarded as best will of course change. The context for prayer will also change, as our lights to God cease being blocked by capitalist Babels and aggregations of Babels in Babylon. Marxism also offers, possibly for the first time, a material grounding of that vision and the obstacles contradicting its realisation in specific human systems. Marxism could not have been formulated without a material base in technology and social relations which had raised the stakes in human history and possibility discontinuously higher than they had ever been before. The situation which led a thinker like Robert Owen to talk realistically for the first time in human history of the abolition of poverty was a necessary precondition of Marxism, and that situation gives the vision I am referring to its reality, but not its inevitability. Taught by Christians to think dialectically, Marxists see 'the knife edge of the present' and how we make history 'not quite as we please'. At their best they see (and they are at their best no more often than Christians) the specific obstacles to the universalisation of the best: the way in which the future is contained as a kind of kinetic energy in the present, but how any one future is not inevitable until it has happened, and has to be mediated and shaped through us and our labour and our associations. Marxists try to see behind the outward and visible signs of society – enclosure, factories, automation, international conglomerates, states, systems of government – an inward but accessible logic. It is a logic of process or, rather, of struggle. The formulation and the status, once articulated, of this logic remain and will remain disputable. Nothing is so disputatious as a group of Marxists talking about their own central theoretical categories, except perhaps a group of Christians talking about theirs. As James Connolly, a catholic Marxist and activist remarked, 'we could not claim to have a mission to emancipate the human mind from all errors, for the simple reason that we were not and are not the repositories of all truth'.[18]

The important thing is to be part of this discourse, or at least part of the subjects which constitute it and to which it refers. The important thing is to have the courage to try, to try to shape our dreams – but grounded in human possibility (with which Jesus's mission and what happened to it had, to put it mildly, something to do with disclosing) rather than being grounded in money, price and profit. The important thing is to dare to be human fully and universally, created as we are by God not as wholly subordinate satellites but as, in some sense, Daughters and Sons. To paraphrase Samuel Smiles, what some men (even One Man) have been all men could become.[19] But to dare to be human using our reason as well as our aspirations. Putting it mildly again, all I would suggest at this stage is that unless we come to grips with concepts like Value and how it is created, Commodity and what commodities are and what their place in capitalist cultures has become, the Labour Process and how it is constrained, Capital and how it is accumulated and reproduced, Labour and what power it has and how that power is appropriated and returned to its possessors not as their own..., unless we come to grips with these and related concepts, we shall have no hope of shaping one preferred future (the one which embodies *our* idea of human purpose or indeed *any* idea of human purpose) rather than another. Coming to grips with such concepts does not mean repeating formulations about them by rote. It means daring to think what specifically Christian contributions might be, for example about the means/ends relationship and the virtue of prefigurative forms as a social/political strategy. Or about the relationship between form and substance in social/political change. It means entering as Christians – in order to help to develop and change – a quintessentially human enterprise, rather than rendering to Caesar so much that the things that are God's become unintelligible and, in the forms they assume *because* so much has been rendered unto Caesar, unattractive and irrelevant to most people.

References

1. This chapter is a truncated version of a paper first written in June 1976 and specifically addressed to my fellow trustees of the Christendom Trust. Since then it has been used and helpfully criticised, in a much longer version, in annual Consultations the Trust promotes – consultations between the Maurice Reckitt Fellow in Christian Social Thought at the University of Sussex, the Trustees and others interested in developing Christian thought broadly within a Christendom Group tradition. Enquiries about the Christendom Trust to: R Minney, College of St Hilda and St Bede, Durham DH1 1SZ.

2. John Kent reflects on this period in the chapter of this book 'From Temple to Slant: Aspects of English Theology 1945-1970', pp 73-82.

3. cf the opening of chapter 1 of *Religion and the Rise of Capitalism.*

4. V A Demant made a courageous stab at answering this question in his Scott Holland lectures published as *Religion and the Decline of Capitalism,* 1952.

5. I tried to face these two questions more explicitly in sections of my 1976 Christendom paper which had to be cut for the purposes of this book. Available from Robin Minney, Secretary of the Christendom Trust. This is also the topic of my book, *Religion and Voluntary Organisations in Crisis,* 1976.

6. See, for example, R Currie, *Methodism Divided: a study in the sociology of Ecumenicalism,* 1968, pp 189-90; or Bernard Watson, *Soldier-Saint: George Scott Railton,* 1970, pp 121-133.

7. 'In all forms of society there is one specific kind of production which predominates over the rest, whose relations thus assigns rank and influence to the others. It is a general illumination which bathes all the other colours and modifies their particularity. It is a particular ether which determines the specific gravity of every being which has materialised within it.' Karl Marx, *Grundrisse*, 1857-8, Pelican edition, 1973, pp 106-7; or *Capital*, III, 1894, Chicago, Chas Kerr edition, 1909, p 521.

8. C Silvester Horne, *Pulpit, Platform and Parliament*, 1913.

9. For a marvellous plea for a contextual understanding of associational forms, in this case the political party, see A Gramsci, *Selections from the Prison Notebooks of Antonio Gramsci*, eds Q Hoare and G Nowell Smith, 1971, pp 150-1.

10. The Brighton Labour Process Group, a fraction of the Conference of Socialist Economists (CSE), has been working on these matters: cf *Capital and Class*, no 1 (1977). A necessary book on any prophet's agenda would now be H Braverman, *Labour and Monopoly Capital: the degradation of work in the twentieth century*, 1977.

11. R H Tawney, 'The Abolition of Economic Controls 1918-1921', in *Economic History Review*, XIII, 1943, pp 1-30.

12. E J Hobsbawm, in *Industry and Empire*, 1968, p 208, calls the British war economy during the Second World War 'the most state-planned and state-managed economy ever introduced outside a frankly socialist country'.

13. W H Beveridge, *Voluntary Action: a Report on Methods of Social Advance*, 1948; and *The Evidence for Voluntary Action*, 1949.

14. I have tried to do this for 'Apathy' in 'On the Uses of "Apathy"', in *European Journal of Sociology*, XV, 1974, pp 279-311.

15. My ideas on this are at a very preliminary stage. But see Stephen Yeo, 'Working-Class Association, Private Capital, Welfare and the State in the Late Nineteenth and Early Twentieth Centuries', in Noel Parry, Michael Rustin and Carol Satyamurti, *Social Work and the State*, Edward Arnold, 1977, and 'State and Anti-State: Reflections on Social Forms and Struggles from 1850', in P R D Corrigan (ed), *Capitalism, Class and State Formation: Historical Investigations*, Quartet Books, 1980. For lucid exposition of 'the contradiction between potential and performance' in the 'riddle' of the English proletariat as observed by Marx, see Philip Corrigan, 'State Formation and Moral Regulation in Nineteenth Century Britain, unpublished PhD, Durham, 1977, pp 84-86.

16. See Maurice Reckitt, *P E T Widdrington: A Study in Vocation and Versatility*, 1961, for the break with the Labour Movement and the Church Socialist League Tradition during the six or seven years after 1918.

17. Raymond Williams and E P Thompson seem to me to be contemporary Marxists trying to develop Marxism as intellectual *practice* in very exciting ways – although neither of them would agree with much in this chapter.

18. *The Socialist*, May 1904.

19. At the 1978 Christendom consultation Professor David Jenkins of Leeds University and the William Temple Foundation put a central Christian insight something like this: 'Nobody's going to be human until everyone's going to be human. It's impossible to be me unless everyone can be them, and that is about being us...' He will forgive me if I've got his exciting formulation wrong. Chapter 10 of Rudolf Bahro's *The Alternative in Eastern Europe*, 1979, puts this insight in a very different dissident Marxist-humanist setting.

11. A View from Latin-America

J. M. Bonino

'External views' do not go a long way in understanding human situations.
Yet, on the other hand, one can say that there are scarcely any totally
'external' views on any significant human situation today. Conditions
interpenetrate and shape one another across seas and continents. In the
following pages I shall simply be introducing a few observations on the
'theological activity' in the UK from the perspective of a Latin American.
Yet even that is not for me – and this accounts for the unscholarly use of
the first person singular – a totally 'external' reality. Thus, a word of
personal 'testimony', in the old British Methodist style, may not be
entirely out of place.

My early Christian life is closely associated to Britain. Out of the first
20 years of my life, 14 stood under the pastoral care of British ministers –
my birth, my first instruction, my baptism, my confirmation, my vocation
to the ministry were undergirded by that stern yet personal and caring
discipline of traditional British Methodism. This simple personal story is,
of course, but the reflection of the larger one: British economic influence
in Argentina from the time of Emancipation until the late thirties.* A
missionary from Britain was my pastor, but an executive from Britain was
my father's boss in a British import company. My deeply felt gratitude for
the former cannot blind me to the connection between the two.† But this
track would lead into another story!

British theological influence during my theological education was

---

* There are several excellent treatments of British influence in Argentinian life. A
  particularly brief and perceptive one is H S Ferns, *Great Britain and Argentina in
  the 19th Century.*
† Early in the 19th Century, the great Methodist leader and theologian Richard
  Watson was expressing his admiration of the workings of a Providence that made
  it possible for Britain to export overseas 'not only our bales but our Bibles, not
  only our merchandise but also our missionaries'. Semmel, in his *Methodist
  Revolution,* has very aptly described the birth and significance of this symbiosis.

confined to some scholarly work on the New Testament which some professors forced down our throats. As time went on, I have had a chance to visit Britain for a few days several times and to live there for a few months. It is too scanty a knowledge to entitle me to express 'a view'. Perhaps the only excuse is that our Latin American horizon of understanding may help to ask some questions which the British themselves might find useful in reaching their own 'internal view'. I will confine these observations to the theological enterprise.

From time to time, the echo of a theological 'hit' from Britain is heard throughout the whole theological world. In the fifties we read with great interest the rigorous application of linguistic analysis to the theological discourse. In the sixties Robinson's *Honest to God* immediately found a market in the Spanish language and a place in theological discussion. Hick's (edited) *The Myth of God Incarnate* has not elicited here the same passion that it has elsewhere but it is also known and discussed. Thus, from time to time, British theology stirs the waters although the movement usually does not last long and few of these best-sellers find their way into the classics of theology.

But we cannot dismiss this phenomenon just like that. Why do these books appear? Why are they so eagerly and passionately discussed? What do they have in common — if anything? The answer is fairly obvious: at different levels and in different ways they all try to reconceive and restate the content of the Christian faith in such a way that it will 'make sense' to modern (British) man and respond to his/her deepest needs. This 'modern man', in turn, is usually conceived to be a 'secular being' who has rejected a magic view of the world, who operates on the basis of scientific (or technological, or functional or pragmatic, according to the view) rather than metaphysical reason, who has found a permanent address in this 'saeculum' and this earth. The immediate reception and the fierce discussion seems to indicate that the need for such a reconception and restatement is widely felt. The rapid eclipse seems, alas, to indicate that the old purpose to 'speak of religion to the cultured among its despisers', as Schleiermacher put it almost two centuries ago, has not yet found adequate fulfilment. We shall have to return later on to this question.

We all know, of course, that these sporadic appearances of theological products in the public market are by no means the substance of the continuing theological activity that goes on every day in Great Britain. Nobody working in the field of New Testament, or Patristics, or Church History in general can afford to ignore the detailed, painstaking and solid work of British scholarship in these areas. Perhaps Bishop Robinson himself is the best example of both aspects of British theology, the careful and sober research of the New Testament scholar and the bold and brilliant adventurer in reconception and communication. Those outside

Britain should be glad to express our gratitude and to acknowledge our
debt both for the solid scholarship and for the challenge and stimulation
that British theology provides.

During the last 10 to 15 years Latin America — as it is now widely
known — has enjoyed (or suffered) a much-debated theological
'renaissance'. It did not emerge originally from the theological milieu
itself but rather from the ministry of the pastors and priests who are in
daily touch with the struggles, the hopes and the miseries of the people,
particular of the poor. Their main questioning had to do with the
function (the *performative* role) which the Christian religion actually plays
in the life of the people. They demanded that the theologians become
aware of this reality and that they relate their work to it. In other words,
they asked the theologians to become responsible for the *effects*, the
actual operation of their work. They invited us to ask ourselves: who are
we? what are we doing? whom are we serving? These are questions that
have to do, not merely with the contents of theology (though this has also
to be examined!) but with the 'process' and the 'conditions' of production
of theology. We have found these questions revealing, although at times
deeply disturbing. I shall simply try to raise some of them in relation to
British theology. Of course, it is for British theologians to say whether
they are helpful at all and to provide the answers.

The first question has to do with the *subject* in the theological
enterprise: who does theology? Obviously, the theologian is not an
isolated individual. His immediate frame of reference is — so it seems to
me — the academic community. The questions with which he deals are
usually articulated from within this community; the conversation around
those questions takes place within it; the frames of interpretation are those
current in it. To the extent that this is true, there are at least two related
questions that deserve to be examined.

On the one hand, how is the academic community related to the wider
Christian community, to the people whose existence (as Christians) makes
theology possible at all? In order to answer this question one would have
to canvass some hard basic information: who are the people that 'consume'
theology at the further end (the pew, the bookstore, the religious
broadcast) and how do they relate, in terms of social status, of
consciousness, of motivations and concerns, to the academic community
that generates that theology? I do not have these data. When I have
attended religious services in Great Britain, I have most frequently found
small attendances of what seemed to be middle or lower-middle class. The
preaching was in most cases informed by traditional pietistic theology or
moral exhortation, sometimes also reflecting social concern. But, on the
whole, it was my impression that the theology developed in and by the
academic community was not very significant in the everyday life of the

Christian community.

On the other hand — and not unrelated to the former — we should ask what is the relation of this 'subject of the theological enterprise' to the total British society. Again, we would need the assistance of some basic sociological information. The recently published *Britain Today and Tomorrow,* under the sponsorship of the British Council of Churches, collects some interesting data in a chapter called 'Poverty and plenty'. The net result of the investigations into conditions of birth, education, income, work, health, housing, wealth ... and even death in different sectors of the British population suggests, in relation to our question, that the academic community represents a very limited sector of the population, mostly located within the upper classes and to a large extent self-perpetuating. We need not adhere to any doctrine of mechanistically conceived conditioning of consciousness by class-belonging in order to recognise that, under these conditions, there is bound to be a significant difference in outlook, expectations, mental representations, between the academic community and the larger society.

In other words, and putting it rather crudely, one could say that the answer to the question: who does theology? and for whom? is: a limited sector of a social class (the academic community mostly located in the middle and higher-middle class) does theology basically for the same community. To the extent that this answer is true (and I would only venture it as an hypothesis), one of the basic problems for theology would be how to relate the theological enterprise actively to the larger Christian community and to society as a whole. This does not mean (we must caution against a false conclusion that has already caused some damage in our situation) a lessening of the scholarly concern or disregard for the academic community, but it does mean that unless theology finds a way to overcome class captivity, it cannot expect to render a true service to the 'whole people of God', either within the Churches or in the wider social body.

A second question follows from the first: who is this 'secular man' whom the academic community conceives as the addressee of its reconception and reformulation of the faith and why does he seem to remain (on the whole) insensitive to those efforts? Sociologically speaking, we must answer that this man is the *bourgeois,* ie the middle sectors that developed in the cities with the birth of the capitalist system of production and the industrial revolution. We know that on the whole (although less in Britain than in the European continent) the workers lost their interest in the Church and are 'low consumers' of religion.* On the

* The story of the 'class-consciousness conversion' in movements like early Methodism (of which Wesley himself was aware) is worth pondering. Again, I would point to the work of Semmel, who sees Methodism as incorporating an important section of the British population to the 'modern' world.

other hand, the 'modern secular' ideology has come to pervade the consciousness of most other sectors of society. It is therefore very important to understand the place of religion in this ideology. In very succinct terms, one could say that the understanding of religion presupposes the clear distinction between a 'public' and a 'private' realm in the life of people. All life is built on the foundation of this distinction: the 'private life' must at all costs be protected against any invasion by 'the public'. Connections between the two can only be made through personal morality (integrity and honesty in work, responsibility as a citizen, even generosity in relation to the less privileged). But no structural relations can be established between the two.

Now, religion definitely belongs, within this ideology, to the private realm. It nourishes, ensures, strengthens the inner life and the immediate sphere of shared privacy (the family). It spills over into the public sphere insofar — and only thus — as it builds personal morality. In order to understand what this means, it is important to realise that this distinction between public and private runs through the life of each individual: there is a necessary participation in the public (work, politics) to the extent that it creates the conditions in which the individual can emerge into his own, private life. When this is applied to religion, it tends to equate the 'private' with the 'inner', subjective (frequently called 'spiritual') life. Religion has its own particular and separate sphere within the private domain. Certainly, this proper function of religion is variously interpreted. But the distinction of realms (the public and the private, the external and the inner, the material and the spiritual) remains the fundamental presupposition. Any attempt to tinker with it meets with a visceral reaction because it endangers the bourgeois' whole understanding of himself and the world he has built.

The attempt of the theologian to overcome this dichotomy is understandable but seemingly doomed to fail. He would like the 'secular' man to integrate his religion within the same horizon of understanding in which he moves in the 'saeculum'. This the secular man will not do. He does not need religion to help him to operate in the world. He needs it — if at all — in order to compensate, in his *private* life, for the effort, the frustrations or the sheer lack of meaning of his 'public' life. What he expects is that religion will 'satisfy' him, not that it will transform him. He does not need 'explanations' but a feeling of comfort, security, inner satisfaction. This is the reason — it seems to me — why the theological attempts to reach the 'modern man' cannot in any way compete with spiritualistic and charismatic movements, esoteric cults or even magic and occultism. All of these have understood better the 'function' of religion for modern man. Insofar as he is 'secular', modern man does not need or want a religion. Insofar as he needs and wants it, he must have it outside the 'saeculum', in his private and inner life.

Thus, this desacralising theology seems sociologically and psychologically inadequate. It seems to me that it is also theologically questionable. In fact, it frequently absorbs, perhaps unconsciously, the 'absolutistic' stance of the bourgeois, modern man. The bourgeois is a man closed upon himself: he takes control of his world, establishes relations which he regulates according to his interests and purposes. But at the centre of his life he remains absolutely in control of himself; he is self-sufficient. His ideal is to be invulnerable. When theology tells him that he can accept the Christian faith from within his 'secularity', it is in fact confirming this stance, including God and Christ within this set of relations which are within his control. This is usually done by means of moral (whether personal or social) transcriptions of the Christian message. But this is precisely what the Gospel will not tolerate: the God of the Bible will not be made into a manageable image — an explanation, a law, a religion: he will remain the Living One that calls and acts from outside us and our 'controlled world', who will never be just a function of ourselves. And this, not because he is himself a 'bourgeois', self-sufficient being writ large, but because his 'divinity' — like our 'humanity' — consists precisely in going out of himself, in being vulnerable, in relating to someone who retains his freedom and running the risk of that always threatened relationship. Insofar as theology accepts the 'secular man' and the 'secular understanding of the world' as they have developed in our Western culture from the time of the rise of capitalism, the Enlightenment and the industrial revolution, it condemns itself to offer a truncated gospel which can only confirm the truncated humanity which a man-in-himself and a class-for-itself have created.

There is a point, nevertheless, at which theological interpretations have, at least in principle, broken through the ideology of the 'self-sufficient bourgeois': the primacy of love which, in different ways and under different concepts, is underlined in most of these theological attempts. In fact, the human essence is frequently defined as love and the active exercise of the latter as the only possibility for authentic human fulfilment. One may wonder, though, whether that same theology realises how radical and far-reaching are these assertions when they are seen against the background of the ideological captivity that dominates the society in which the theological enterprise takes place (and particularly the sectors of that society which participate in the production and consumption of theology). For this ideology, in fact, love can only be another activity of the sovereign individual or a feeling of sympathy strictly confined to inter-personal relations. The Biblical concept of 'love', on the contrary, presupposes a going-out to the 'other', an openness to one who remains 'other' and therefore represents a challenge, a risk and a danger. It is significant how frequently Jesus has to select the 'offensive' other in order to convey the meaning of God's love and of real human love (the 'publican', the prodigal son, the leper, the Samaritan). But in order to do this, 'modern middle class man' would have to undergo a true ideological and class conversion. He would have to give up his identity as the 'private', self-sufficient individual that he is and to become public and vulnerable, both within his own society and in relation to others in the world. This can scarcely be done simply in the intellectual realm, within the sphere of theology as such. The 'locus' of that conversion has to be a real encounter with that 'other', a praxis (if I may use the much abused word) in which the actual breaking through of the private self-sufficient individual takes place. This is a miracle of the Spirit which theology cannot contrive. It can point it out as a promise and it can reflect on it as it happens. The question for theology in Britain (as elsewhere) may well be this simple one: where is this happening? where is it happening in the community of Christians and in the larger human community? There, a theology which has broken through class- (race-, sex-, ...) captivity may really be born.

These last remarks are not meant as pious exhortation or as a theory about theological progress. They are simply the expression of our Latin American theological experience of the last 10 to 15 years. If one abstracts from that experience a more or less general formulation, it could be done as a reflection on 'the subject of theology' — who does theology? Traditionally, it could be said that there are at least four instances within the Church as the subject of theology: the gathered Church (mainly in the worship); the 'teaching Church' (those officially commissioned to teach, from the Sunday school teacher to the university professor of theology); the 'charismatics' (those who vocationally reflect and teach, whether officially commissioned or not, the prophet, the philosopher, the reformers — be they individuals or groups); and *the Christian people* who live out their faith (whether consciously or unconsciously, faithfully or not) every day. For us in Latin America the rediscovery of this last instance has been decisive: in their expressions, their actions, their struggles and sufferings, the people manifest an understanding and a dynamics of faith (whether we evaluate it positively or negatively) which is frequently much more determinative for the appropriation of the Christian faith than the official teaching of the Churches. In the last analysis it is the cultural transmission of this popular piety, the mutations that it suffers through the historical circumstances, the interaction of this piety with the special ministries of the Churches that determines the face of Christianity and its 'performative' significance at a given time in history.

For us, this 'people' is the marginal, oppressed, silent masses, those 'banned from history' who in their strange 'religious dreams and fantasies' frequently give expression to that deep rebellion against 'reality as it is', that stubbornness in persisting in living against all odds, that trust that somehow the 'divine' must be on their side — against hunger, sickness, unemployment — which is at the heart of their faith. It is true that their religion is frequently alienating (how could it be otherwise if their whole life is alienated — possessed, used, determined by an alien, another, the oppressor?). It is also true that we run the risk of 'theological populism'. But it is more fundamentally true that the awareness of this fact has led in Latin America to a new 'pastoral' mission, the attempt to help the emergence, among this mass, of communities that bring into their consciousness the meaning of their faith, of the gestures and expressions, which actualize the liberating potential of their Christianity. One hundred thousand 'basic communities' in Latin America are already a new 'subject' for theological reflection!

Thus, a new ecclesial reality is being born as the matrix of theological renewal. It does not obviate the need for 'academic' reflection. But it establishes a new task for it. It is not any more a self-enclosed and autonomous instance which has itself as reference. It now has to respond to that new ecclesial reality in a triple way: as offering an articulation of theological and social analysis which may give historical substance to the struggle of the poor — the provision of an interpretative frame of reference; to continue the basic research — Scripture, history — with the new-gained freedom which helps to uncover the hidden, ideological, class-bound presuppositions and prejudgements of much that passes for purely objective scholarship, and thus lay the foundation for reinterpretation; finally to help to organise the relations of that multifaceted 'subject' of theology in terms of the new priority. Certainly, all of this throws us into the dilemmas and contradictions — and therefore the risks and uncertainties — of potential conflict. But it also offers the possibility of a creativity which, we hope, may not *simply* be the reflection of historical circumstances, but *also,* and at the same time, part of those 'new things' that the Spirit of Christ has yet to teach us.

STYLES

12. On Looking Back into the Future

Rex Ambler

There is, as far as I know, no political theology that is related specifically to the situation in Britain. To understand the reason for this state of affairs would be an important part of any attempt to develop such a theology. It seems to me that such an attempt is desirable for the reasons that have inspired its development in other countries: primarily that the truths of Christian faith cannot be realised in practice without an awareness of the political and social conditions in which we live. But I also believe that the theological task is so demanding and so far-reaching that any initiative in that direction can only be tentative. What I want to do here then is to offer some programmatic suggestions for a political theology in our own situation.

It is not possible to import, for example, the Theology of Liberation from Latin America. That theology has been worked out precisely as a reflection on the distinctive situation in Latin America and is therefore by definition 'not for export'. But it challenges our theology nonetheless: it calls at least for a reconsideration of the historical and social basis of British theology. It might even be said that the sense of history — that sense of live history which understands the present in terms of the whole life of the past and of the future which it makes possible — is precisely what gives this Latin American theology such immediate relevance and political force. It is clear, at any rate, that no theology in Britain can hope to match the political and social issues of our time which does not rediscover a sense of our own peculiar history and of the special role of Christianity within it.

Historical moments

Many of the peculiarities of British life are derived from the fact that Britain pioneered the development of the modern world. It led the field early on in the evolution of nationalism and democracy, but also at a later

stage in the industrial and technological revolutions. It had time to adapt
slowly to their profound social consequences and so was able to retain an
almost unique sense of continuity with the past. The other side of
Britain's stability and continuity, we should note, is its marked inability
to keep pace with the most recent changes in the modern world. It is
perhaps what a pace-setter should expect, that eventually, inevitably, he
will be overtaken by others. But this early start in modernisation also had
a specific effect on religion, and was in turn affected by it. The ironical
aspect of the interchange, as I want to show, is that while religion
'facilitated' these historical developments, in the outcome it lost some of
its power to shape political life.

Nationalism was facilitated by the Reformation in the 16th century.
Henry VIII could appeal to the Reformers' criticism of papal and
ecclesiastical authority in severing England from the dominance of Rome,
though the reasons for this break were not wholly religious ones. The
result, however, was that the English king, rather than the Pope, became
head of the English Church. Religious and national independence was
bought at the price of the Church's submission to the state. It was
therefore Queen Elizabeth I, and not the archbishop, who supervised the
fateful compromise between protestant and catholic faiths and laid the
foundations for the present Church of England.

Democracy was established, at least in principle, in the Commonwealth
of the mid-17th century, and partly as a result of the egalitarian ideas that
had been fostered by the radical reformation and fervently practised by
many groups that had supported Cromwell in the civil war. The
Commonwealth was too unstable to last. But in the Restoration of the
monarchy after 1660 a new compromise was worked out which allowed
two elected parties, the Whig and the Tory, to have an increasingly bigger
say in government affairs. Yet the political ideas of these parties had
already lost their grounding in religion: it was the rationalist Locke rather
than the biblically minded Milton who set the tone for their debates.[1]
Why? Because, to the minds of the rulers, religious politics in Britain
meant civil war and insurrection. The success and failure of the revolution
of the 17th century meant that the Church of England had lost the power
to convince and control the people – and therefore the power to
legitimise the state – but also that no alternative religion was able to fill
its place. So in the late 17th century the state withdrew its enforcement
of religious conformity in the Act of Toleration and gave public
recognition to the fact of religious pluralism. Once pluralism is accepted,
as Peter Berger has shown,[2] the issues of public life begin to be
secularised and religion becomes increasingly a matter of personal choice
and concerns itself increasingly with private life. From 1740 onwards the
secular philosophy of the Whigs is complemented by the evangelical

message of Wesley.

The industrial revolution was a triumph of technological reason, but it
would hardly have been possible without the faith in individual initiative
and worldly asceticism which had been encouraged by the Reformation. In
its turn it created the secular ideology of free enterprise while preserving
the theology of personal piety, at least among those people who were free
to benefit from material expansion. However, the masses of the people
were being uprooted from the traditional life in which established religion
made sense and thrown into the anonymous and insecure world of the
new cities. The new chapels helped some of them, but the majority were
as alienated from religion as they were from the industrial processes they
were forced to serve.[3] The evangelical revival of the mid-19th century
spoke to the conditions of men who found themselves lost in a
competitive and fast-changing world, but it did little to alleviate their
material distress. It was left to the labour movement, supported by the
secular ideology of socialism, to give substance to the hopes of the new
industrial workers. If Methodism and Dissent provided the initial
inspiration and organisational structure for the leaders of the movement,
they played little part in its development which became more and more
secular as more and more workers became involved in it.[4]

Once again, working class culture reflected, even while negating, the
culture which dominated it. At one time, in Dissent, it had echoed the
Reformed theology of the dominant Church. Now, in socialism in the 19th
century, it echoed the secular bourgeois philosophy which advocated
democracy, liberty and self-improvement, though, according to the
socialists, only for the privileged few. Yet the secularism of the labour
movement was more an indifference to religion than a conscious
opposition to it — religion had already played itself out as a political and
social force. This is perhaps one reason why the militant secularism of
Marx and Engels found little support in Britain — it had been worked out,
intellectually, in the context of German and French politics where the
established churches still played a dominant role. In Britain Christians
could and did take part in the labour movement without too much sense
of incongruence. At any rate, this *partial* secularisation of British life,
which applies both to socialism and capitalism, meant that no powerful
and coherent and integrated ideology was possible. Also, the continuing
and accepted pluralism of British religion, reinforced in the late 19th
century by the stalemate between church and chapel,[5] prevented any
effective use of religion in support of a political stance. (This applies less
to Scotland and Wales where presbyterianism and nonconformity,
respectively, were integrated with a sense of nationality and were not
seriously rivalled by alternative religions.[6]) For lack of ideological
coherence British politics became pragmatic — 'secular' in the weak sense

of leaving all religious or ultimate questions out of account.[7] It also
became less polarised than the politics of Germany and France. It allowed,
for example, for important compromises between labour and capital,
pragmatic agreements about wages and welfare, which both improved the
lot of the workers and eased the political conflict.[8] It made the way for a
universal franchise and a democratic state based on consensus.

Imperialism in the 19th century was a policy of political domination
intended to protect the supply of cheap goods and labour and a market
for manufactured goods in undeveloped countries. It was a necessary
development of the home policy of industrial expansion and relied on the
same secular philosophy of free enterprise. However, as at home, it was
accompanied by a religion of fervent evangelicalism, in the form of the
missionary movement. Missionaries followed the paths and railways of
capitalist traders to offer the gospel of personal salvation. Except in India,
where religion and culture were resistant to the West, they christianised
large sections of the empire, often more successfully than in Britain itself.
As imperialism declined, after the first world war, Christianity in
undeveloped countries took on independent forms, often combining with
movements for national independence and cultural renaissance. With the
final collapse of imperialism Britain has experienced an influx of
immigrants from the old colonies, with a rather different religion from the
one which it knew. Among the old chapels and churches we now have
pentecostal meeting houses, mosques and Hindu temples, and we are
beginning to relearn what fervent religion looks like.

The technological revolution was pioneered by Britain at least in
respect of armaments, chemical industries (eg ICI) and television (BBC). It
created an economic boom in the fifties and sixties, but since it relies on a
rapidly increasing consumption of technological goods its economic
benefits would only be temporary. The anti-bomb protest of the sixties
reflected a widespread awareness of its inherent dangers, as the student
protest of 1968 reflected an awareness of its cultural banality. Marcuse's
One-Dimensional Man, which gave the theory for that protest, also spoke
more widely of the cultural effect of a society geared almost exclusively
to rapidly increasing consumption. He described it as a society in which all
the options in life were available within the present system, because they
could be bought. Television, along with other technological media, has
penetrated private life to provide many of the satisfactions that were
previously found in church or chapel — it provides ideology and
entertainment, everyday drama and ritual sport in which people feel they
can participate, but also a sense of national and social unity, a sense of
being cared for and a sense of taking part in a world more significant than
one's own. That nearly religious sense created by the media is in one
important respect illusory — the practice of watching television, listening

to records, going to the cinema is itself passive and receptive, and involves no real participation in what is seen and heard. It is a form of alienation which allows very little room for the development of an alternative society, even in the imagination, However, the soothing tones of the media, like the services of the established church in an earlier age, have little to offer people who are radically dissatisfied and frustrated. In our society it is the frustrated adolescent, the disillusioned immigrant, the little man with no prospects, the lonely old-age pensioner and widow who turn enthusiastically to religion. Religion now plays no vital part in the culture of either the working masses or the educated elite who manage them. It is a voluntary option that is relevant to specific social groups whose sense of personal identity is being eroded, rather than established, by the dominant culture.

The future of religion

Are we then, as Bonhoeffer thought, moving towards a time of no religion at all? I doubt it. The history of religion in Britain has not been that of a steady decline.[9] Religion has never, so far as we can tell, been embraced by the majority of the people. But it has at various times been embraced and sometimes enforced by the dominant group in society, and it has become the battlefield of conflict between groups contending for dominance. It has now played out its role as a political ideology, partly because the conflicts in religion have been unresolved and partly because its hopes and promises have to some degree been fulfilled in a secular form, for example in the movement towards democracy and economic equality. But its hopes have not been fulfilled for everyone, or completely fulfilled for anyone. So for those who are still close to the minority tradition of Christianity it will continue to play at least a compensating role in personal and social life. It is quite possible that as times get harder, as the economic crisis begins to disrupt our longstanding social stability, this personal religion will have a revival, as it did in the mid-19th century. But there is an alternative future which for some Christians still is much closer to the historic impetus of Christianity. In this prospect Christianity can and should be embodied in a prophetic community, accepting its minority role but relating its specific religious practice to a wider secular practice for the transformation of society. The present powerlessness of the Church in Britain can be thought of as an advantage. It means that the Church is not compromised, as in other countries, by a close alliance with the forces of reaction. It is free to move in the political field because it is not so firmly lodged there as a part of the establishment. And in some places, eg among students, alienated blacks, disenchanted priests, it is free to adopt radical and progressive causes, to apply its own tradition creatively to the task of constructing a human socialism. This is already happening, on a small scale, and there are chances of more and more Christians being involved in it in future. But at least one question remains to be settled: how is our understanding of Christianity to be developed if that is to be possible? What creative changes are required in theology if Christianity is to assume a prophetic role in British society?

Memories and hopes

The symbols of Christianity come from a distant past, expressing ancient memories and ancient hopes. They have accumulated new meanings as they have been appropriated at later times to express newer memories and hopes. In this way, like other religious symbols, they enable people to transcend the present and the immediate past, with their confusion and suffering. But they remain ambiguous because they can always be appropriated in either of two ways: as providing primarily a memory of a time when men's hopes were once realised – symbols of a past and therefore permanent fact – or as providing primarily a hope of a time that was dreamed of in the past – symbols of a future and as yet unrealised possibility. In the first appropriation the history of Christianity is the history of the discovery, and loss, of what was originally given, so that any more recent formulation of the faith can be regarded as definitive. In the second appropriation the history of Christianity is the history of the partial realisations, and betrayals, of its promise, so that *no* past formulation can be regarded as definitive.

Christianity in Britain today is mainly of the first type. It is preoccupied in its practice with the evocation of a fact of the past, the incarnation of God in Christ, and with the implications of this fact for the experience of the Church. Its main formal practices are preaching, in which given truths in the Bible are rediscovered and restated, and the administration of the sacraments, in which the historical Christ is in some way realised in the present. Its social and ideological structures are usually taken from some definitive moment in the 17th or 18th century, which then mediates the more distant moment of the Christ event. There are of course many variations of practice and differences of emphasis between and within the Churches, but it is not over-generalising to say that the intention of most Christian practice is to actualise in the present what was originally given in the past. This tendency is reflected in theology, which becomes most serious, and contentious, in Britain when it deals with the nature of the historical Christ and the form of his presence in the Church. The intensity of the debate on the recent book *The Myth of God Incarnate* indicated where the interest of most Christians lay.

This feature of Christianity is not to be identified with that characteristically British respect for tradition, though it may be the case that, with the increasing nostalgia in this country, the two have been mutually supportive. Respect for tradition as such can supervise fundamental changes. It has progressive possibilities. Respect for the religious tradition must be part of Christianity in any form; every definition of Christianity would have to make some appeal to the historical Christ. And in some of its forms, eg in the sects of the 17th century, it has been able to use that appeal as a lever for progressive change. In the present form of mainstream Christianity, however, the appeal to tradition is essentially retrogressive. Christianity undergoes change, as it tries to adjust to prior changes in society, it does not implement change in the future interest of society. It is not that it has tried to implement change but failed, but that it has not found it in its interest to try. The point of reference for its own self-identity is not in the future but in the past.

It would appear then that a fairly radical reinterpretation was called for; and the question of how we appropriate the past is crucial here. We do not have to cling to the past in order to benefit from it. Nor do we have to construct an unchanging essence of Christianity which survives all historical change. On the contrary, we can recognise that the significance of the message in the past was precisely its meaning for the history in which it was expressed. The original message of Jesus was unmistakably about 'the time' in which he lived and the time in the future he passionately hoped for. The interpretations of people who followed also had their meaning, whether consciously or not, as responses to the history through which they lived. It is only by recognising this that we can begin to understand why interpretations of Christianity have changed. And it is only on the basis of this that we can understand how Christianity might be developed creatively to meet the challenges of our present history. In other words, the Christianity of the past should be relativised in order that the Christianity of the present can be free to respond to the realities of the present, but also that it might be free to draw, creatively, on the whole history of Christianity in making that response. If that appears to call in question the basis of Christianity and to ignore or deny its historical continuity, it could be said that its basis might be in a continuing history and that its continuity through time might have more to do with the quality of its response in each phase of history than with its formal adherence to some earlier definition of belief or practice. There is, we might say, a progressive concept of continuity as well as a regressive one: namely, the concept of a continually changing response through social and cultural change which represents the same fundamental stance towards change. What this stance is in concrete terms would have to be defined differently at different times, in terms of a relevant practice. But it can also be described generally, in terms of those traditional symbols and symbolic stories that pervade Christian history. It is, we could say, waiting and working for the Kingdom of God, it is dying and rising with Christ, it is living in the spirit of the age to come.

Living in the future now

But what is this stance in contemporary Britain? If it has to be a response to our own time in the light of the time we hope for, we have to appreciate both the specific challenges of our historical situation and the universal challenge of a future 'kingdom' that bears upon us morally in every lived moment, both in love and in the desire for liberation.

Part of our historical situation — a rather fundamental, determinative process — is the development of the capitalist economy in a time of international economic crisis. And part of this development is the very specific effect of a strong labour movement, of an expensive system of welfare and social benefit which derives partly from that movement, of a systematic intervention of the state through nationalisation and investment, of the loss of world markets to more successful competitors. All this, in giving shape to the economy, has profoundly affected the situation of employment, bringing many more people into the pay of the government, and the situation of unemployment, which is beginning to sow seeds of political discontent. The centralisation of power, both economic and political, is bringing many more people into the experience of alienation and powerlessness, while at the same time it is creating a broad common interest in the transformation of the structure of power. More and more professional groups, for example, are becoming unionised and identifying themselves, economically if not culturally, as a new working class. Also women are becoming much more involved in the national economy so that their inherited social position is being experienced increasingly as oppression; they too can identify themselves as a new working class with an interest in a struggle for power. Blacks and Asians, having moved into Britain with some hope of betterment, are now discovering the rigidities of the British caste system, which, like other such systems, needs some identifiable group at the bottom. The Scots and the Welsh are experiencing the centralisation of power in another way, as undermining their national identities and freedom. Historical grudges are growing into political determinations. Yet these and other processes, which stem from changes in our capitalist development, cannot be understood wholly in terms of that development. They have also to be understood in their own specific terms, as social rather than economic processes, and in terms of those cultural processes which inform people's hopes and attitudes. I have referred already to the cultural effects of television. We could also take account of the growth of education in the last 30 years, and of both its liberalising and domesticating effects.

Is it possible, then, on the basis of such an analysis, to discern a process of liberation in the long term that might in turn suggest a specific social goal for British society? There would need to be more detailed analyses and more specifically political discussion before we could answer that convincingly. I can only suggest that if this account is on the right lines so far, we can discern a process of concentration and centralisation of power, and another process, in reaction against it, which is pressing for the dissemination and decentralising of power. We are witnessing a phase in the development of capitalism in which the blind forces of capital are working demonstrably against the real interests of the majority of people. The economy can evidently be humanised only if it is broken down into manageable units and managed democratically by everyone involved in it. If the economy is left more or less as it is, it will grow — towards a more unified European and then Western economy and it will be 'manageable' only by a comparably large political state. A socialism which merely tampers with the economy, which cares about the distribution of wealth but not about its acquisition, is failing to tackle the roots of our present social crisis. What is needed in Britain is a movement for socialism which aims at the full participation of workers in their work and people in their government. That is both a viable political project and a desirable and necessary step in the liberation of British people.

It is inevitably a *political* project since the projected changes involve a transfer of power and a transformation of the uses and sources of power. But it is more than a political project, since the movement to implement the changes (successfully) must arise from the people themselves and requires great resources of awareness, insight, sensitivity to others, personal sacrifice and courage in action. The failures in attempts to build socialism in this country and others are well known. They are due, among other things, to the use of political means that belie the socialist end. Socialist movements have failed to *be* socialist in their style of operation. They have therefore also failed to engage the majority of the people, and where they have led to a seizure of power they have had to maintain power by repressing the people. These failures are understandable if we recognise that what is called for in a successful project is an anticipation in the movement of the values that the movement is struggling for. The future that is hoped for has to be held in the imagination and so far as possible put into practice in the struggle to realise it. This very paradoxical demand is actually implict in any social project which aims at a qualitative change. The future that is hoped for will either be created by those who hope for it or it will not occur at all.

Part of any socialist project in Britain which engages the people in a creative movement is the specifically *cultural* project of releasing human energy and awareness. We need efforts in education, art, music, drama, literature and science that will at least counteract the prevailing ideology

of resignation and nostalgia, and give us something to hope for. And part
of this cultural project is the specifically *religious* project of evoking a
very long memory to awaken a transcendent hope. The religious project,
in Britain, cannot be identified with the wider *historical* project since, as
we have seen, religion no longer plays a dominant and determinative role.
But it can be part of that project since it draws on a memory that is still
importantly alive and anticipates a future that is otherwise easily
forgotten. In particular it can serve that project by making its practice
prophetic, rehearsing the tradition of prophecy in a struggle for, and
witness to, the promised peace and justice, maintaining its characteristic
stance in relation to the present situation. It can give a depth of meaning
to the historical project which it would not otherwise have, whilst in the
same process it can establish its own meaning in a particular historical
situation.

But what, again, is the distinctively Christian stance? Has it in fact
already been eroded by this rigorously historical view of the meaning of
Christianity? Is there after all no special dimension of faith? The
horizontal dimension of history is all we need, I suggest, at least initially.
For there are different ways of living history, of experiencing time. To live
by the clock, so to speak, realistically and pragmatically, is only one way
of living time. It is also possible to live in the past (as I have argued many
Christians do) or to live in the future in the light of the past (as I suggest
we should). To live in the future can of course be an evasion of the
present — unless the hoped-for future is prefigured in the present, for
example in the attempt to create that future. This peculiar stance of living
the future now, in the light of its previous lived anticipations, is a way of
overcoming, of transcending, the regular process of time which both
erodes our achievements and delays their fulfilment. It reaches out
beyond the limited present in order to return to it and live it creatively. In
this way it gives a meaning to our lives and a substance to our hopes that
would not be available to us from a purely realistic account of our history.
It is therefore most naturally expressed in images. The imaginative
reconstruction of our history, which is prominent in certain art forms like
drama, novels, films and folk song, gives us a sense of time and history
which matches some of our deepest feelings and longings, and therefore
gives us a richer sense of ourselves. It links our personal project with a
social and long-term historical project, and as such it is a necessary
correlate to the more scientific and analytical understanding of history
which provides the realistic context for our action. The particular value of
religious conceptions and practices is that they establish some ultimate
points of reference for our actions, a sense of a beginning and end to the
human story. But precisely because of this they threaten also to displace
us from the world of real history and create the illusion that that

imaginary story is real history. When that happens of course they undermine the creative impulse to change the real world, and religion becomes reactionary. But when religious consciousness is combined with a realistic consciousness, as consciousness of real possibilities in the real world, it has a powerful liberating effect. It telescopes history so that liberative moments of the past and liberative possibilities of the future can be held vividly in our minds when we undertake the tasks of the present. It keeps hope alive by recalling the end in our preoccupation with means.[10]

Christian practice, like Christian language, is deliberately symbolic. It expresses the end in the means, recapitulates the whole human story in specific actions and styles of life which give meaning and impetus to the rest of our lives. They can be none the less real for that. To love one's neighbour is both an anticipation of a society which has yet to appear and a creative action in the real world. But it does not by itself create the society in which love becomes a universal possibility. For that we need means that are suited to the social realities of the existing world. The paradoxical nature of love is expressed in the classical Christian symbolism of the passion and resurrection of Christ. His creative love is destroyed by a loveless world, but vindicated in the outcome. Love then is an eschatalogical act, as Paul indicates in I *Cor* 13: 'Love never ends; as for prophecies, they will pass away.' Or, if you like, it is dialectical, because while affirming the humanity of men it negates existing human relationships and is in turn negated by them — in crucifixion. It awaits its realisation in a world so transformed that it is beyond our conceptions to grasp.

References

1. cf. Perry Anderson, 'Origins of the Present Crisis', *New Left Review,* 23, 1964; eg pp 28, 30: 'Because of its "primitive", pre-Enlightenment character, the ideology of the Revolution founded no significant tradition, and left no major after-effects. Never was a major ideology neutralised and absorbed so completely. Politically, Puritanism was a useless passion.' This somewhat overstates the matter, as E P Thompson shows in his reply, 'The Peculiarities of the English', *The Socialist Register,* No 2, 1965, reprinted in his book, *The Poverty of Theory,* Merlin Press, London, 1978.
2. Peter L Berger, *The Social Reality of Religion,* Faber, London, 1969.
3. cf Friedrich Engels' description in his *The Condition of the Working Class in England in 1844.*
4. cf Eric Hobsbawm, 'Religion and the Rise of Socialism', *History and Humanism,* an issue of *The New Edinburgh Review,* Nos 38-39, 1977.
5. This is the main theme of A D Gilbert's book, *Religion and Society in Industrial England: Church, Chapel and Social Change 1740-1914,* Longman, London, 1976.
6. cf Daniel Jenkins, *The British: their Identity and their Religion,* SCM, London.
7. This is Denys Munby's *Idea of a Secular Society* (OUP, London, 1963),

which, though not intentionally, is a typically British idea.

8. cf Alasdair Macintyre, *Secularisation and Moral Change*, OUP, London, 1967.
9. cf Peter Burke, 'Religion and Secularisation', in Peter Burke (ed) *The New Cambridge Modern History, XIII, Companion Volume*, CUP, London, 1979, pp 293-317.
10. My thoughts in this paragraph have been influenced by Ernst Bloch, *Man On His Own:* John S Dunne, *The Way of All the Earth;* and Alfredo Fierro, *The Militant Gospel.*

13. Doing Theology

John Vincent

I. Doing Theology in Context

'Doing Theology' is a process whereby elements of Christian faith 'go to
work' or 'come alive' or achieve new meanings and implications, within
the realm of this or that specific area of human concern.

Theology itself is best seen as the constantly multiplying 'end results'
of people in this or that situation taking some aspect of the Christian core
of faith and discovering new ways in which the truth as it is in Jesus can
be lived and witnessed to. Very few theologians ever sit down and say,
'Now, let's think up a new doctrine'. Few of the most useful theologians
sit down and say, 'Now let's think of a new way to put someone else's
doctrine'. The true theologian says, 'How does the Gospel itself come
newly to me, where I am, with my own questions and presuppositions —
and to my people, those with whom I live, and move, and have my being?'
Theology is a 'given', a constantly expanding given, but still essentially
'from outside'. All theology is thus no more and no less than the record
of the constantly varying ways in which this or that element in the core of
faith is utilised, or realised, or enlarged, or contracted, within the compass
of the demands and obligations of particular disciples in particular times
and places.

This is not to say that theology is socially or politically 'determined',
but simply is to say that theologians do not say things simply because they
are true, but because they are true in relationship to some issue or issues,
some consciousness or situation, some mood or concern, some
presupposition or assumption, within the cultural, political, social,
economic and religious situation of their own time. This can easily be seen
by comparing the images and lives of Jesus, through history; or by
comparing what 'justification by faith' has been taken to mean or imply
in different times and cultures.[1]

This becomes very clear when the context is the arena of politics —

politics being understood as the way in which the secular life of cities, areas and nations is organised and governed, and the way in which all people affect that organisation and government.

'Political theology' is 'doing theology in the context of politics'. Political theology is the result of taking seriously the special questions and situations of the political realm, the utilising of aspects of Christian faith to serve some kind of response. The response of any political theology itself will always be partial, not merely because of the personal and social uniqueness of the theologian doing it, but also because the areas of 'politics' and of 'theology' are also both essentially partial.

In the political context, any work must be partial, and therefore, any political theology will always be partial and temporary. It will depend heavily upon the place the theologian occupies in the culture, the society, and the political situation. It will depend upon the race, nation and community the theologian is with. It will depend upon those to whose questions the theologian takes it that there is a call to provide answers. It will depend upon the political options and, to the same extent, the political theories which are around at the time. It will depend on the 'hunches' the theologian has, quite apart from any theology. It will depend on the party political allegiance, if any. It certainly will depend on who pays the theologian, for what, and what is done with the money which is received. All of these are decisive at the political end.

This partiality at the political 'end' is, in fact, matched by a like partiality at the theological end. It is not a matter of applying a whole, agreed, static, body of truth, called 'theology'. Rather, it is a matter of juggling with very disparate and sometimes mutually contradictory elements from the theological storehouse. Inevitably, the theological predilections of the person in question, the denominational positions of the churches and the philosophical fads and fancies of the time will influence the theologian. There is no way in which the theological elements can be other than partial.

'Doing Theology' in the context of politics is the process of bringing together these disparate bits and pieces from the side of the political situation and from the side of theological and scriptural understandings. Usually, it is not a question of simple 'snaps' or 'matching-up'. It would be easier if it were. It would be easier if one could equate political socialism or communism with New Testament 'all things in common', or attitudes to the state with 'the powers that be' in *Romans* 13; or the poverty-stricken masses with Jesus' 'Blessed Are You Poor'. But any of these equations do violence both to contemporary political realities and also to the meaning of the theological elements within their own contexts in the New Testament.

Therefore, it is necessary at times to hear the political and the theological, as far as possible, in separate and comparatively 'pure' form. This we now attempt to do.

II. Political Elements

It does not seem to me to be necessary at this time to rehearse again a 'Christian' apologia for liberalism, conservatism, Marxism or socialism. This is far too much like the common mistake of theologians baptising the baby after it has already grown up, or claiming the horse after it has already bolted. Faced with the available political options of our time, few Christians will be greatly helped by one more appeal to adopt this or that political stance, join this or that political party, or adhere to this or that political philosophy. Especially, it seems to me, a belated rallying of the Christian forces to the Marxist perspective is mistaken. Partly, this is because Marxism, like capitalism, belongs essentially to an industrial producer society, and we now need to be thinking of the next kind of society we want. Again, Marxism is already too biased a tool to be flexible enough to deal with present realities in our 'mixed' economies. Finally, it is at least arguable that there is a Christian or Catholic method of social organisation which is to be preferred to either the capitalist or the socialist ones.

Be this as it may, it is my own experience that those who adhere to political philosophies are sometimes less useful when it comes to actually doing battle than those who tend to work on more 'do-it-yourself' models. My own essays into political areas, at any rate, lead me to this conclusion. It did not greatly assist, as I recall, when we were trying to get nuclear disarmament, that some of our number were committed Marxists. Nor yet does the record of the early discussions on the evils of racism indicate that ideological presuppositions or commitments necessarily excluded racist attitudes.

Partly as a consequence of this, my political engagement over the last 10 years has been in relation to urban affairs. Here, time and again, one has experienced so-called socialist parties in power in city halls behaving like landed gentry. Equally, one has seen the powerlessness of trade unions to act in any but a conservative way in the face of new situations or demands. And, needless to say, the existence of a few Marxists or socialists in the university or in the white highlands of West Sheffield has made no difference whatsoever.

I have claimed earlier that the decisive elements in any political commitment — as in any thological commitment, as I shall shortly show — relate to the place a person occupies in a society, to the community around, the questions being heard, the style of life being shared, the source and use of earned income and so on. My own perspective and situation are those of a Methodist minister, paid by local people in inner-

city Sheffield to help with small local white and black churches for one
third of my time, and paid by fellow ministers and laity and by
denominational and ecumenical bodies to run a mini-theological seminary
of the streets for two-thirds of my time. I live in a cosmopolitan road of
Edwardian semi-detached houses, down the road from the house in which
the theological unit is based.

We have often had an interesting check-back on our own perceptions
by visitors from outside who come to our 'Come Down our Street, Lord'
weekends. Among early items on their timetable is either 'The
Grimesthorpe Pilgrimage' or 'The Pitsmoor Pilgrimage', conducted by my
colleague, City Councillor Francis Butler. Sometimes when they return, I
ask them to list what they have seen. The list usually runs something like
this:

> In places, an air of deprivation.
> Small surviving communities.
> 'Ghettos' of middle class whites, or West Indians, etc.
> Several racially integrated neighbourhoods.
> Many old people in single dwellings, often segregated.
> Many children in certain neighbourhoods.
> High-rise or barrack-type flats in separate areas.
> Desolation in recently demolished sections.
> Proximity to heavy industry.
> Houses or other buildings used as churches.

Inevitably, the discussion turns to the question, 'Why are things like
this?' At this point, it is inevitable that I turn to my own experience to
'explain' things: and that experience inevitably turns to theology also as a
way into the way things are, and the way they could be different.[2]

III. Theological Elements
If such are some of the political elements in my situation, as I see it, then
I see myself as called and privileged to be able to bring to those elements
some additional understandings, based upon theology. These additional
understandings, hopefully, will eventually provide some 'leads' or some
value-judgements or, conceivably, some illuminative parallel stories and
even some alternative models and some alternative policies; however, we
must first attempt to hear the theological elements 'on their own', as we
did the political ones. But the task is not easy or straightforward.

How, faced with an urgent, if chronic, situation, in which I daily
participate, and whose disadvantages and joys are daily with me, can I even
begin to hear theological elements faithfully? Or even hear theological
elements at all? When I open the Scriptures, I shall look with the eyes of

my own person, with all its limitations and assets. I already know too much! I am already too deeply committed! Moreover, I have already staked my life on a few bits from the theological storehouse and taken a chance that a few others can be left till later! How can I then come to obedient listening to the strangeness of the Bible, or parts of it — or of theology, or parts of it?

Much comfort is to be derived from the fact with which I started this paper. There never has been any writer of Scripture or writer of theology whose vision and message were not addressed to the context of the day, which means determined and shaped by the political, economic and cultural situation of the time and place in which the writer was living. Recent New Testament scholarship has emphasised the point. Students of the Gospels now speak not only of the necessity to discover the situation of the early Church and the way its life, points of view and political, social and cultural commitments might have influenced the way the words and deeds of Jesus were passed on (Form Criticism). The importance is now also stressed of recognising the peculiar political, social and cultural presuppositions and stances of the different Gospel writers themselves and how such factors might have influenced the way they wrote (Redaction Criticism).

Thus, I go to Scripture or theology with my involvement-laden agenda, my deep commitment already within some part of my contemporary world, and my place beside certain people and over against certain other people. But I meet in Scripture and theology others whose involvement, commitment and place were no less decisive. So I take courage! Indeed, precisely this 'contextual' character of Scripture and theology provides me with some clues as to how I must proceed. Let me illustrate this by suggesting some procedures, using the first three Gospels — the parts of Scripture we find most useful in Sheffield.

1. *Find a Writer with a Similar Political Context.* The New Testament bears witness to a wide variety of political, cultural and social situations. Paul was a Jew, but also a Roman citizen, and found it convenient to evoke his Roman citizenship at times, and thus advised others to 'respect the powers that be' (*Romans* 13, v 1). The writer of the book of Revelation, probably a Jew in a Gentile church, lived in a time when the Roman rule was hostile to Christians and thus called for Christian resistance (*Rev* 14, v 9-12) (or chapter 18). The Gospel writers came out of very different situations, usually understood today as follows: Mark is addressed to people tempted to think that 'the end of the world' has come because of the terrible events of the time. He probably wrote in AD64-70, and *Mark* 13 refers to the Jewish revolt in Palestine and the Roman seige of Jerusalem. Matthew is addressed to Christians who need to create their own political and cultural separateness with their own Rules and

Commandments and Institutions. He probably wrote around AD75-80, reflecting the need for Christians to create their own 'third nation' after the emergence of a separate, exclusive Judaism at the Council of Jamnia, a Judaism of the synagogue after the sacking of the Jerusalem Temple in AD70. Luke is addressed to Gentiles who need to discover their long-term friends among the Romans – the Jews are now the enemies and Christianity is the true Judaism. Luke-Acts was probably written around AD75-80, to demonstrate that the present development of Christianity in Gentile lands was part of the plan of God for all humanity's salvation.

Thus, 'politics' for Mark is a matter of keeping people out of premature or unnecessary commitments. Typical is his saying of Jesus, avoiding taking sides between Rome and the Temple. 'If the coin has Caesar's head on it, give it to the Romans. If the coin is a temple coin, use it in the temple' (*Mark* 12, v 15-17). For Matthew, 'politics' is a matter of establishing the new political community, the Church, separate from Judaism. For Luke, 'politics' is seeking a *modus vivendi* within the Roman empire.

So, one way to do political theology is to ask to what Gospel your situation is nearest. If your situation looks like the end of everything, then go for Mark; if it needs a new community and discipline, then go for Matthew; if it needs to be good witnesses in a pagan but hopefully benign environment, then go for Luke; if you are in a society which does business with ideas and philosophies and world-views, then John's Gospel might be helpful. Thus is set up, based on a 'snap' between the two elements, a dialogue between you and your own situation and the Scriptures.

2. *Discern the Variety of Political Responses Available.* This way, you do not begin with making a 'snap' in 'identification' between your own situation and one of the Gospels. Rather, you try to sort out the available options and choose between them.

Certainly, Jesus Himself chose between the available political responses of His time. He could have sided with the Zealots – indeed, the events of the feeding of the five thousand was very probably an attempt to make Jesus into a leader of a Zealot uprising. He could have sided with the Sadducees and the cooperators with Rome – but He was finally condemned by just such people. He could have stayed with the group with whom He had the most natural affinity, the scribes and Pharisees, and urged the people to leave politics to others and concentrate upon personal piety and religious obedience – but this seemed to Him the way of hypocrisy and legalism.

3. *Study the New Option Jesus created.* What in fact Jesus did was to create His own option. He created an alternative community of 'cross-bearers' (like the Zealots), He urged people not to make trouble with the Romans (like the Sadducees) and He urged His disciples to follow strict

rules (like the Scribes and Pharisees). But His underlying purpose separated Him from all these options. He was basically creating a new community discipled to Himself and to the Kingdom of God.[3]

The most significant political act of Jesus was the calling and mission of His disciples. Twelve of them He apparently called the tribal heads of a new political entity, the reconstituted Israel of His own followers. He sent them out to preach, teach and heal – to imitate Him. The political reality of the Kingdom was a dynamic new possibility, existing already wherever certain kinds of things happened. The disciples could not 'build' the Kingdom, but they could indicate its reality by word and deed. The Kingdom was thus not something which 'grew' progressively. Rather it was something which appeared, suddenly. You could perhaps embody it for a moment, but not possess it as continuing actuality. The Parables are the indication of the Kingdom but never lead to any 'definition' of the Kingdom, any continuing tangible organisation or entity.

What Jesus did, then, was to set up an alternative political reality, the Kingdom-discipled community. This new political reality related to the existing political realities of Judaism and Rome only in terms of expediency. If the State is in turmoil, keep your head down (Mark). If the State builds barriers, build barriers yourselves (Matthew). If the State can be won to be benign, cooperate with it (Luke). But none of these attitudes is of prime importance. They are strictly matters of expediency. What the disciples have to do is to protect, propel and, if possible, embody the Kingdom of God, which came into unique existence in Jesus Himself. The 'political' task was, therefore, the task of trying to preserve the reality and the possibility of the Kingdom, and at times symbolically embodying it in some 'acted parable'.

4. *Face the Apparent 'Irrelevance' of the New Option.* The alternative political reality of the Kingdom-discipled community does not, of itself, have any political power in the secular sense. In New Testament times, if a Christian disciple were also a Roman soldier, or a slave-owner, or a slave, or a tradesman, or a teacher, or a commercial traveller, or a landowner, or a housekeeper – then he or she would have to work out the implications of a Christian commitment within the possibilities and limitations of the job – or change the job. In post-New Testament times, there emerged suggestions as to certain jobs which were inappropriate or impossible for Christians – such as prostitute, soldier, money-lender or temple employee. Few early Christians had to face the problem of the possibility of exercising significant direct political power or holding significant political office.

As is well known, this was changed under Constantine in the years after AD312, when Christianity became the official religion of the Roman Empire. My first introduction to this was reading the famous chapters 15

and 16 of Edward Gibbon's *Decline and Fall of the Roman Empire,*
Volume I, when I was a schoolboy. I still think that Gibbon had a point
when he blamed the Christians for the Empire's decline. Christianity ill-
fitted the role of political power and has similarly not achieved great
success in those times and places since then when groups of Christians
have attempted to translate Kingdom-Community into local political
reality (examples would be the Anabaptists in Munster, the
Commonwealth in England, the early settlers in the United States).

Thus, Christianity is not a directly applicable political 'solution' or
'policy' capable of being established and maintained in a society or nation
as a whole. Jesus did not intend it as such and it has not been a great
success when it has been tried.

5. *Face the Limitations of 'Christians in Politics'.* The failure,
inconsistencies and impossibilities of the 'direct' line has encouraged
many Christians to believe that the 'Christian' contribution is to be found
simply in ensuring that there are good, honest, conscientious and generous
Christians at work in various parts of the political machine, in local and
national government, in political parties, in the judiciary, the police, the
welfare services, the educational systems and so on.

However, this apparently unexceptionable procedure has all too often
merely affirmed the status quo. At worst, it has oiled machines which
ground people down in injustice; at best, it has kept going with moral
people situations which were themselves amoral. The great army of
devoted Christians who have done public good is not in question: how
they actually functioned as members politically of the alternative
Kingdom-Community is very much in question. That there should be
good people in public office is undoubted. And that Christians are often
among the available good people is excellent. But at the end of the day,
the Christian committed to participation in someone else's political party
is going to have to vote with the party. The residual Christianity of third
or fourth generation Methodists and Roman Catholics in the British
Labour Party in the 1980s is a welcome fact. The existence of any
continuing reflection or reference back to the Christian faith is, however,
more notable by its absence than by its presence. This is undoubtedly
because the Churches, as the guardians of the faith, are busy at almost
everything other than serious and enterprising concern with the present
implications of Kingdom-reality. But equally, the politicians who began
with Christian commitment have long since satisfied themselves that
really to get on with the political business, the philosophy they have
adopted — conservative, liberal, socialist or Marxist — is far better 'got on
with' by itself, without endless and often fruitless discussion with
Christians back home at the ranch. As President Nyerere advised, 'Seek
first the political kingdom.'

IV. Some Ways Forward

So, which way now?

Somewhere, there has to be an explicit and intentional development of the Christian notion of the Kingdom-Community as it impinges upon political realities. What we have said so far makes a cautionary tale. But that is not to say that the task is not worth pursuing, or the possibilities for new development not still there. I believe five lines are open to us, derived essentially from the plurality of situations (1 above) and the Jesus option (3 above). I have been concerned in this essay with trying to provide some kind of semi-theoretical way to speak of Doing Theology as a style of Political Theology. In this last section, I can only briefly refer to things people can follow up elsewhere. There has, fortunately, been more 'doing it' than 'theory' so far.

1. *'Mix It!'* I believe that the possibilities for progress lie somewhere in the area of 'doing theology'. They exist where faithfulness to political elements and faithfulness to theological elements come together. They exist where something in the political 'sparks' something in the theological or where something in the theological 'sparks' something in the political. They exist in the 'mix' that happens when contextual and theological elements are put into the same 'crucible'.

The processes whereby this takes place are many and varied. Suffice it to say that Urban Theology Unit has laboured with many models and methods and is not satisfied with any of them. But we remain convinced that it is the vital issue. In New York recently I was discussing with Dr Bill Webber his own attempt to 'do theology' in the city. 'Well, let's just say it is *the* most important thing,' he said, 'how you bring theology and context together. If we ever got *that* right, we'd really be swimming.'

Let me merely report on one such method, by taking up again the story of our 'Come Down Our Street, Lord' weekend groups. Often, I go straight into a piece of Bible study, after they have listed the characteristics of the area as they have seen them. I invite them to look at chapters 2 and 3 in Mark's Gospel and ask them quickly to list some of the things they see going on there. They supply a list like this:

Paralysed man healed through friends' help (2, v 1-12)
Outcast traitor becomes disciple (2, v 13-14)
Meals with collaborators and lawbreakers (2, v 15-17)
Unsocial behaviour by disciples (2, v 18-28)
Holy day conventions broken (3, v 1-6)
Crowds of outsiders, deprived people (3, v 7-12)
Small community created (3, v 13-19)
Family division, controversy, blasphemy (3, v 20-35)

Then I say to them, 'Are there any bits in this list which are anything like your first list?' So, we try to play the game of 'Snap' or 'Happy Families', matching up if we can a contextual 'card' with a Gospel 'card'. Lines get drawn from one list to the other, labelled:

Deprivation	Alienated people	Racial mixing
Ghettos	Small communities	New Community

Now, we are 'Mixing It' between the Inner City of Sheffield and the little towns of Galilee.

2. *Make New Community!* Invariably, we then get into a discussion about vocation. 'Do you have to go to live in the inner city for Gospel things to happen?' someone asks. 'No, but it helps,' someone replies. 'Is the only hope to create small communities like you have in the Mission?' another asks. 'What then do I have to do?' 'Should I go into politics?' 'Should I be a social worker?' 'How can I be a minister?' In a moment lives are up for grabs, defences raised, policies settled, doors opened, doors slammed tight. Gospel has become politics – for politics begins in call and community, in context. The 'mix' has begun, with context and theology as ingredients and everyone's future as the crucible.

The most crucial political decision, in my experience, has been the decision as to where to put oneself, with whom to put oneself, in what style to live one's life. The first political act must be to obey what one hears to be a call, and to become incarnate in some place. And no one can be incarnate on their own – much less engage in healing, exorcism, proclaiming the Kingdom, embodying the new community, witnessing to the reversal of all things, being constantly open to new calls from the Gospel. The call to Gospel obedience is the same as the call to Gospel community-building. For without it, the whole Gospel agenda is rarely faced. I am not sure that the contemporary Christian community movement is in much shape to realise its political potential, but that perhaps merely means that we now need some Kingdom-style communities of specifically political intent.[4]

3. *Act Parables!* The first disciples were called to be 12 in number as a 'sign' to Israel; to hail their Leader on a donkey; to shake off dust from their feet to expose people's hostility; to cast out devils to show the Kingdom power; to imitate their Master in action and word; to pluck corn on the Sabbath to indicate the law was at an end; to fast or not to fast as they wished; to give up their possessions and have things in common; to go swiftly from place to place without encumbrances. All of these were actions, but also parables. They indicated what they also momentarily embodied – the Kingdom in which all things were different. They were acted parables, prophetic signs.

Recent instances could be given — fasts, political demonstrations, sharing of possessions, creating a walking-distance community, starting an Acts Cooperative, moving a church into a shop, creating 'alternative planning' training, running a wholefood store with unemployed staff.[5] Wherever humanity has become 'stuck', not knowing where to turn, it is good politics to get on and act an alternative parable. The world might even notice and move over.

4. *Prophesy!* Last and certainly least, the Kingdom-discipled community speaks!

There are occasions to speak — many of them. But speaking must always be on the basis of a real striving to face Gospel and politics together; it must be out of a committed contrary community whose life gives credence to prophecy; and it must be on the basis of things that can be seen — acted parables.

But occasionally, prophecy is in order. We have had our say on World Development, Planning, Education, Community Relations, Theological Training.[6] Sometimes kind and generous church leaders come to Abbeyfield Road. They tell us, confidentially, that the small Gospel communities are the hope of the Church!

The Archbishop of York, Dr Stuart Blanch, joined us for a consultation on the two Archbishops' call to the Nation to debate 'The Society We Want'. After a day together, we felt we had something to say on the basis of our context and our theology. We wrote:[7]

'The Archbishops' call raised questions about the sort of society we want and what kind of people we want for that society. The response so far assumes that what is wrong with our society is that it is permissive, lacks law and order, is workshy and is heading for economic disaster and social chaos. Therefore people propose that we need more control, more family life, more security, more stability, more hard work and healthier positive attitudes.

'We feel that society is wrong for different reasons. We therefore have different proposals. To us, these things are based on the life and teaching of Jesus.

Five main concerns
'1. The Archbishops say "Every Man and Woman Matters". But we believe that the key people are the people our society regards as insignificant — the poor, those disadvantaged, educationally, racially and socially.

'Therefore we want a society which continually lends itself to give special consideration to the disadvantaged, whoever they are.

'2. The Archbishops say "The Family Matters". But we believe that many of the good aspects of the Family have been tragically weakened by assumptions that people have to move away to get on, or that everyone must get as high a standard of living as he can, or that people can be moved by planning, or that independence and privacy are more important than community and interdependence.

'Therefore, we now want a society in which everyone gets grandparents, mothers and fathers, brothers and sisters, and children, even if they are other people's.

'3. The Archbishops say "Good Work Matters". But we believe that to work well on what is not worth doing is worse than not working at all.

'Therefore we want a society in which work is useful to others and fulfilling to the workers, without being detrimental to others or to resources, and within which everyone has their share of dirty and boring tasks, and has roughly equal rewards.

'4. The Archbishops say "The Other Fellow Matters". But we believe that in our unequal and distorted society, certain groups have to struggle for a better place even though it is to the disadvantage of some people who already have what they need.

'Therefore we want a society in which people learn how to respond imaginatively to the needs of others, in other countries as well as other situations.

'5. The Archbishops say "Attitudes Matter". But we believe that people's attitudes are determined by nation, class, race, standing and money, and that these have so far not been challenged.

'Therefore, we want a society in which the elevation of people because of money, position, race, education, social standing, or tradition, is so eroded that alternative attitudes based on love, humility, cooperation, consideration, self-denial and mutual affirmation are made easier.'

References

1. The sociological, cultural and political histories of Christian theology remain to be written. Initial forays may be pursued in Robin Gill, *Social Context of Theology*, Mowbrays, 1975, and *Christian Theology in Society*, Mowbrays, 1978.
2. cf my *Into the City*, Epworth Press, 1980.
3. cf the article of Roy B Crowder on the Ashram Community House in Sheffield (above, pp 38-42). On this whole section see Edward S Kessler, 'A Jubilee and Disciples', in *Stirrings: Essays Christian and Radical*, ed Jonn J Vincent, Epworth Press, 1976, pp 47-68.
4. cf David Clark, *Basic Communities*, SPCK, 1977.
5. For some of these, see John J Vincent, *Festival for the Future Church*, Ashram Community Trust, Sheffield, 1979.
6. For papers on these issues, contact the Urban Theology Unit, 210 Abbeyfield Road, Sheffield 4.
7. 'The Society We Want', in *Doing Theology in the City*, Urban Theology Unit, 1977, pp 16-17.

14. The Church as an Agent of Social Change - from the Edge

Thomas Cullinan O.S.B.

Many years ago Mario Borelli described to a packed town hall at Oxford his work among the *scugnezzi* boys in Naples. When he had finished a voice from the hall asked: 'And what is the Church doing to help?' Mario laughed. 'That is a very British question. I am the church.'

A very British question, indeed, because Anglo-Saxons are over conscious of their institutions, structures and systems. Whether, in a particular case, we happen to be for them or against them, we overestimate their potential. If *for* them we expect them to carry us and to solve our problems; if *against* them we blame them for our impotence. In either case we take them too seriously.

Institutions and social structures are part of the fabric of human life. Always they are both good and bad, just and unjust. They both enable us and constrain us. But they never exempt their members from responsibility.

The Church is an institution. It cannot be otherwise. To accept the mystery of God as revealed and incarnated in a living community of men and women is to accept that the Church is an institution; and also to accept that she will always be more or less ambiguous in revealing that mystery in concrete terms. For her to be *in* the world always means that she is more or less *of* the world also.

The consciousness and the daily lives of Christians, clergy and laity alike are always conditioned by the society in which they live, always participate in and contribute to the sin-impregnated norms of thought and behaviour which currently prevail. Those who have tried to escape this by working for a Church of the Holy have always ended up irrelevant and righteous.

Because of her messy and ambiguous character, the Church cannot *as a whole* ever be ready and poised to read the signs of the times, nor to be sufficiently free in society to be an agent of radical change on behalf of the poor. For one to complain that things ought not to be so is like complaining that one ought not to be a sinner. We are flesh and blood, not angels.

Two thousand years of history should, in any case, warn us not to exhaust our precious dreaming by expecting the Church at large to be ready. And if the evidence of history is not enough there are plenty of contemporary reasons for not expecting it. One would be the soft-mindedness of liberal democratic courtesy. Since there are good men to be found on each side of every political issue, politics is assumed to be neutral in relation to God and His Kingdom. Faith is seen to provide no criteria for political judgement or action. Politics belongs to the realm of secular opinion, not sacral imperative. Church leaders are expected to play a balancing game — a bit here to the left, a bit there to the right, all shades of opinion are valid. Is this not a tacit denial of the socio-political stance taken by Jesus? A stance which led to his death, in a very politically conscious age.

The Church is a gathering of pilgrims. Some have only just set out, others are way ahead; some are walking, others running, some are fascinated by the scenery, others have eyes only for the road ahead; some have a single problem, how to cope with excess baggage, others are relatively free of baggage. There are the mad, the bad and the sad. But they all make up the Church and all need a place. The only thing inadmissible is settling permanently by the roadside and refusing to go on (though which of us do not settle from time to time?).

It is not reasonable to envisage this human motley as a whole being equipped, or indeed free, to read the signs of the times in faith and engage in any serious *praxis* in the light of that reading. The real issues in any social moment are always obscure and responding to them requires a special freedom and courage which do not rely on certainty. This is a minority role. As Thomas More said, it takes 'long leisure and diligent search for the matter' and it takes, too, an ability, or at least readiness, to disengage from vested interests.

The freedom, the space, needed for this is born of an insight into poverty (in both of its dimensions, as personal ascesis and as social fact in the poor) and of an authentic life of prayer. But it also requires a certain space in life to respond in a prophetic sort of way. This is not possible for the Church at large and indeed to suppose that it is may imply a naive fundamentalist idea of the last three years of Jesus' life being a norm for all Christians. Jesus was able to reveal God in the prophetic way he did because he was not married, was not an administrator and had no normal social responsibilities. He did not demand the same of all who followed and it would be a one-dimensional Church indeed if he had.

This is not to say that 'Blessed are you poor' and to be '*in* the world but not *of* it' are not universal criteria for all Christian judgement and life, but it is to say that prophetic *praxis* is a function within the Church rather than of the Church at large.

There is another reason why the prophetic role of being an agent for radical change belongs to minorities within the Church, not to the Church at large. The Church by and large is people by and large, and people by and large do not uncover reality nor locate the latent injustice in their society as long as the goods are still being delivered.

A few weeks ago I asked Bishop Labayan, from the Philippines, whether he thought the Church in this country could clarify her role and rediscover the good news as liberating without an experience equivalent to the fascist oppression in his own country, which had clarified their faith. His answer was a simple and gentle: no.

Twelve years ago, when my own monastery was being pressed by friends in Africa to found a house there, I mentioned to one of them that there was talk of a house in Scandinavia. He replied, 'Scandinavia will not hear the good news as such until a major social crisis has happened. But Africa is ripe now.'

Suffering, crisis, persecution, marvellously focus the mind and clarify issues. People may feel a deep ennui and suffer from profound boredom and alienation, but as long as apparent prosperity lasts those dark areas of experience remain unrecognisable.

A society can be so preoccupied with economic pursuits that the desperate hunger of the alienated self (generated by those very pursuits) cries out for a liberating, meaningful voice of hope, and yet that voice remains inaudible precisely because of those preoccupying pursuits. People are trapped in their limited and fascinating economic language and can appreciate no other. 'I will send a famine on the land; not a famine of bread, nor a thirst for water, but of hearing the words of the Lord. They shall run to and fro to seek the word of the Lord, but they shall not find it.' (*Amos* 8)

So, for the time being at any rate, the Church will be an agent for radical change in what Helder Camara has called her small Abrahamic groups. These are groups of people in any walk of life who by choice or necessity throw in their lot together, abandon what is stable and secure and set out like pilgrims to seek what God is really saying in their concrete situation within our modern society.

There are many isolated Christians who are politically conscious and working in local or national politics, voluntary agencies (like Oxfam), trades unions, many organisations. I have often felt that a great force is being dissipated because they (we) do not appreciate the need for cohesion in generating new language, new understanding and new life. But from whatever setting, be they families, clergy, students, organisations,

Abrahamic groups are essential as growth points within the life of the
Church in modern secular society.

What might we expect of such a group (albeit in an idealised form) as it
journeys, if it is to be both politically real and also faithful to God?

A Prophetic Group

Justice is the name assumed by love when it extends beyond looking after
our own. However great the demands of loving and taking seriously those
among whom we live, one cannot but wonder if Jesus would not have
said: 'What credit is that? You have your reward already. Even the pagans
know how to get on together.'

Love has further dimensions and, as our group evolves a political love
(taking people seriously within the political structures of their lives), it
will find itself carrying the burden of some sort of prophetic vocation.
Hopefully it will discover this with some reluctance and be ever conscious
that self-appointed prophets are false prophets. The burden of prophecy is
laid on a person or a group, it is not picked up by them. As in the Old
Testament the true prophet was known by his identification with the
people in their trials and history, so our group will be authenticated by its
identification with the Church. It will have to avoid self-righteousness,
judgementalism, arrogance and the infantile self-assurance: I'm right and
all of you are wrong.

On the other hand this burden of prophecy, laid on the group as a
result of a political love which most people do not understand, or are
afraid of, will lead to a certain estrangement, loneliness, oddness, even
divisiveness. This apparent distancing is by no means an excuse for the
group to go off and seek its own virtuosity. Paradoxically it is precisely
that distance which renders the group of true service to the Church,
helping to free her from herself. The prophetic group is needed by and
depends upon the body as a whole to a far greater extent than either can
normally afford to acknowledge. The sap wood of a tree is essential to and
dependent upon the heart wood.

A Contemplative Point

Many Christians caught up in radical politics use scripture and the
teachings of Christ as support for their work. But their consciousness and
their *praxis* are not in fact born of a living faith in a living God. They
simply happen to be politically active as well as being Christian. One does
not need to be a Christian to accept Jesus as a moral teacher.

The social and political stance of Jesus was not accidental to his faith;
it flowed out of a contemplative point of union with the numinous and
living God, his Father. Likewise for the radical politics of our group to be
truly faithful it must come to flow from a truly contemplative point. It

is only thence that the group will transcend mere ethical endeavour and come to participate in the mysterious but urgent realisation of God in history among people. This numinous quality will bring hope and urgency to the group while freeing it of concern for itself and its own ideas.

I recall an abbot saying to me, 'Thomas, I would listen to any revolutionary if I knew he spent two hours a day in prayer.'

Anticipating the Dream

There are many who seek radical change but have no feeling for the link between their own way of life and that which they work for. Some even argue that as long as our acquisitive and unjust society lasts one might as well live by its standards. We won't change anything by living otherwise, they argue, and indeed to maintain a voice and have effective contact with decision makers in society, we have got to live more or less as everyone else does.

But our idealised Abrahamic group will anticipate its dream into its own lifestyle and become itself a generator of alternatives. And indeed not only for the sake of generating alternatives but more fundamentally *metanoia*. Both Scriptural and Marxist epistemology agree that our consciousness develops only in dialectic with our *praxis*. *Praxis* covers not only the specific political activity of a group beyond itself, but also its way of life within itself.

If it sees the pampering of acquisitive drives as a root of many other social evils, the group will evolve, however ambiguously, a consumer ascesis in its own life. If it sees competitive individualism likewise, it will evolve a real sharing of resources and communal way of life. By these and other means it will come to that special freedom which knows how to be joyful and serious at the same time, it will integrate its political sense with its faith and it will have an intuitive feel for the mysterious co-respondence between its own personal call to poverty (which is precious to God) and the stark fact of social poverty (which is scandal to Him).

Analysis

An Abrahamic group wishing to avoid becoming a mere get-together and to engage in action which is truly creative needs a constant process of reflection and analysis. Social analysis, that is. It will find itself asking and having to live with questions which lie at the edge of most people's understanding. They lie at the edge precisely because currently accepted language offers no interpretation of many areas of social understanding which nevertheless cry out for interpretation. It is only through the patient determination of groups who will not dismiss such questions as irrelevant or unanswerable that any new language of interpretation is able to evolve.

Of course any radical group must face the temptation of borrowing slogans or cliches from elsewhere and using them to fire its moral fervour. We can learn from others, but no one else can do our job for us. Borrowed analysis relieves our existential anguish by mystification, not by real understanding.

Slogans borrowed, for instance, from early industrial society when the dividing line between owners and workers was the dividing line between dominant and subservient classes do not easily clarify our late industrial society when a managerial class is as deeply alienated as organised labour is bourgeois.

Nor again will liberation theology, as it has recently evolved in Latin America, translate directly into our European situation. We can learn from its methods and approach but cannot avoid having ourselves to go and do likewise.

So our ideal group will face up to the hard questions about property, poverty and social structures in Britain today. Who, for instance, are the poor in our sophisticated society? What is poverty? And how do we listen to God's work for a liberating understanding?

Certainly, in the first place, poverty is penury — inability to cope. And it is no more than bourgeois illusion to think that our welfare society has dealt with all that, or indeed ever can. The prophets of Israel speak to us in our day as realistically as in their own about blindly ignoring those who cannot cope and about the injustice of adding house to house, car to car, holiday to holiday, business to business.

But scriptural understanding of poverty went deeper than mere inability to cope. The poor were those excluded from the normal life of the community, whether by penury, disease, misfortune, or as strangers. If we too understand poverty in those terms we have a clearer way of understanding the poor in our complex and affluent society. I would suggest, as a tool for analysis, that 'the poor' should be understood as (a) those excluded from normal cultural life, and (b) those who are not free to make any significant decisions about their life.

Analysis pursued along these lines will obviously have to face questions about housing, about wages, about unemployment. But it may also face more subtle questions. What, for instance, is the effect within 'normal' society of institutionalising (and forgetting) the 'abnormal' or deviant — Borstals, Old People's Homes, Mental Hospitals, Special Schools?

Or again, what is the psychological and spiritual effect on people, especially in our inner cities, of pressurised consumerism?

In all its analysis and searching the group would have to avoid simplifying questions (and answers) by forms of reductionism; by reducing man, for instance, to economic man. While undoubtedly Marx was right in saying that history is shaped by man's pursuit of the material needs of life (as evidenced, surely, by our present history), it is also true that the reduction of radical politics to mere economics makes it only another cause of the dullness, boredom and lack of creative imagination so widespread today.

The signs of hope today are not found in those who come up with yet another economic solution for yet another economic problem. They are found in those who transcend economics, especially in direct community action enabling people to enliven their low image of themselves, to take life into their own hands.

Finally, if our group is to avoid a sort of nationalism in its thinking, it will need an analysis of how domestic pursuits affect the poor overseas.

Dirty Hands

Our group will also evolve the double art of getting its hands dirty, in concrete political options, and yet not handing itself over to any political organisation.

The former (getting hands dirty) is demanded by faith in an incarnate God, a God who is served not by ideas and clever thoughts but by active obedience on behalf of the people. To keep one's hands clean is in fact to opt for the status quo. But to dirty one's hands always involves ambiguity, uncertainty, risk, which is why many Christians feel there is no imperative to do so. But the fact is that any concrete application of faith is always necessarily ambiguous and uncertain. Otherwise faith is not faith. We are certain of God's presence, of his guidance, of his fidelity, of his promise, but how and when he comes and whether in this line of action or that, we are never certain. But it is only through our engagement in concrete decisions, hand-dirtying decisions, that we are open at all to his guidance.

The latter (refusing to hand ourselves over) comes from a refusal to equate the kingdom with any idealised social model. Or, put another way, it comes from valueing integrity and truth more than loyalty to political party or organisation.

Political option is necessary for political love to be effective in the actual lives of the poor. But no political programmes can usher in the kingdom nor permit our Abrahamic pilgrims to catch a train.

'If faith be the essence of a Christian life it follows that our duty lies in risking upon Christ's word what we have for what we have not; and doing so in a noble, generous way, not indeed rashly or lightly, still without knowing accurately what we are doing, not knowing either what we give up, nor what we shall gain; uncertain about our reward, uncertain about the extent of sacrifice, in all respects learning, waiting upon Him, trusting in Him to fulfil His promise... and so in all respects proceeding without carefulness or anxiety about the future.' (John Henry Newman, *Parochial and Plain Sermons,* iv, 299)

Freedom from Fruits

A living faith in a living God sets a person or group free from over-concern with success. Our Abrahamic group will thus come to speak and to act purely because it has to speak and act. It will not exhaust emotional energies in anxiety about success or failure.

This detachment and spiritual freedom is not an indifference to the outcome of action — for love is only love in so far as it seeks to be effective — but is a profound sense of the outcome of action being in the hands of God. Without such spiritual freedom the group will not find the patient endurance to persevere through setbacks, opposition, loss of friends; it will not be able to give pure attentiveness to the task in hand here and now; it will not discover the precious role of symbolic action; and it will not discover that inner peace and joy which the world cannot give.

Once a group has come to see the peace which the world gives (based on comfort and security) as a sick joke, that sort of peace can never satisfy it again. If it is not to live from then on in a state of anxiety, then it will need a spiritual freedom from the fruits of its actions, and into that freedom God gives his own peace.

Joy

Many who become politically conscious become morally serious, doctrinaire and drab. Their path would lead logically either to totalitarian absolutism, or to despair. Their sense of beauty, their sense of humour, their common sense, all shrivel as victims of moral seriousness. And with those go their sense of the value of ordinary people and everyday life. While desperate to set others free they become unfree themselves, fearful lest the celebration of existence will distract their determination and urgency.

In fact the opposite is true and the Eucharist could become for our Abrahamic group a celebration of life in death, a celebration of freedom which would bring hope, joy and vigour to political endeavour.

'God's freedom is more than freedom from oppression. His new creation is greater than man's past. Resistance must be rooted in hope if it is not to decay into hatred and revenge. And hope must lead on to resistance if it is not to turn into opium for the people.

'The super-abundance of hope can be celebrated only in festive ecstasies. These produce ever new forms of opposition to all forms of unfree life.

'If the liberating feast (the Eucharist) cannot be given a complete historical equivalent in liberation movements, it yet enables us to see better opportunities in the future.' (Jurgen Moltmann, *Concilium*, Vol 2, No 10)

Love

Finally, our group will remind itself often as it journeys, that it does not exist for itself but for others. It exists to realise that love of God for the oppressed, the unloved, the unfree, which characterises the God revealed in Christ. To this concern for people, and to the ultimate demands of truth and love, will be subordinated all group consciousness and loyalty. God is love but not all love is God.

15. The Church as an Agent of Social Change - from the Centre

Pauline Webb

'The Committee for the Defence of the Revolution' proclaimed the poster nailed on a battered door of a back street apartment in Havana. It indicated that inside lived the local secretary of the organisation that has mobilised the entire community of Cuba to participate in the revolutionary process inaugurated 20 years ago by a charismatic leader and his band of comrades. In regular meetings for instruction, in cooperative work brigades, in nightly patrols of vigilance, local committees announce, enact and embody that revolution in every street of the city and every village in the land. Even the revolutionary process requires an institutional presence.

The same might be said in defence of the Church as an institution. Out of a theology of revolution can emerge an ecclesiology of a recognisable form so long as the theology comes first. The problem is that too often the Church has shaped the theology rather than theology being allowed to shape the Church. It is the faith in what God does that should determine the form the Church takes. But since structures have an innate tendency to become prisons in which the very truths they were intended to promote become trapped and obscured, it is tempting to write off the Church as among those institutions of society that are most resistant to change. Yet it is salutary to remember that in their separate histories each of the denominations in Britain owes its origin to a theological eruption in the midst of political and social upheaval. It is when the dust settles over the emerging new shapes of society that religion solidifies again into becoming the cement of the status quo, containing only the fossilised vestiges of its original dynamic life.

But if one believes in a doctrine of a God who is making all things new, whose realm is the whole inhabited earth and whose purpose is the unity of all creation, one can by no means exempt the Church from the processes of change. Rather, from such a theology emerges a concept of a

Church which is not the end-product of the divinely-initiated revolution, but an interim agent towards its fulfilment. The institutions of the Church would then become such as enable people to prepare for, participate in, and demonstrate God's activity in the world. Their mission is to cooperate with all that makes manifest His Kingdom and to expose and confront all that militates against His rule. So, like the Committee for the Defence of the Revolution, the Church too has the job of announcing, enacting and embodying the fact that the revolution has begun. Or, to put it in more traditionally ecclesiastical terms, the Church is called to a three-fold vocation of *kerugma, diakonia* and *koinonia* if it is to be effectively one of God's change agents in the world.

One of the first tasks of any revolutionary movement on achieving power is to announce its presence, to point to the areas over which it has already assumed control and to alert the people to the fact that those powers which may still seem to be determining their destinies have in fact been dethroned. The day of liberation has arrived. Such was the contents of the earliest *kerugma* of the Church. 'Jesus is Lord,' announced the apostles and with that assertion they dared to claim all areas of life as the arena of His Lordship and all other lords as coming under the scrutiny of His judgement. In the light of such a pronouncement, the Church has always then had to decide what posture it will adopt towards the apparently prevailing powers in the context in which it is set. There is no such thing as a non-political Church. As Andre Dumas puts it in his recent stimulating book, *Political Theology and the Life of the Church* (SCM Press, 1978), only the middle classes and the Marxists are agreed in seeing religion as a private affair!

But how does the Church become incarnated in the political situation within which it is set? In Britain there have emerged three kinds of relationship between the Church and the political powers. There are the State Churches which recognise the realities of political power even to the extent of consecrating its institutions and setting Government and Church in a relationship of mutual support and ostensibly, when needs be, mutual correction. The peril of such establishment is that it leads the Church into the temptation to preserve political power and privilege by resisting any movement towards radical change, and involves that kind of identification of Christianity and civil authority which obscures the essential message of the liberating gospel.

The so-called Free Churches maintain the right to dissent from the Established Church and by implication also from the civil powers. Even they have tended to become so conformist to the norms of society that the 'Non-Conformist Conscience', once a formidable opponent of social and political ills, nowadays expresses itself in such a discreet and marginal manner that it rarely disturbs the peace. Strictly speaking, in terms of the

British scene, the Roman Catholic Church is also a Non-Conformist Church since its members do not conform to the Established Churches of England or Scotland but to the Universal Church of Rome. Yet most of them, in Great Britain at any rate, would nowadays profess allegiance to the British crown, and the international dimension of their Churchmanship seems, at local level at least, to have little distinctive effect on their political views as British citizens.

Emerging from all three types of Churches and increasingly finding expression within and beyond the ecumenical movement are groups of Christians with a more radical understanding of the Churches' prophetic role in society. Even at the official level of the British Council of Churches, and in its close cooperation with the Roman Catholic Commission on Justice and Peace, this results on occasions in a critique of British society and the Churches' role in the political realm more searching than the Churches separately might be prepared to undertake. The recent studies on 'Britain Today and Tomorrow' were an attempt at this kind of analysis which at least posed the problems presented by modern society even if they did not come up with many clearly defined recommendations for Christian action. At the unofficial level, Christian renewal movements, para-churches and action groups are taking seriously that confrontation between gospel imperatives and political realities which leads to radical action of the kind that has always characterised the truly confessing Church in every era of history and in most parts of the world.

The Church has been described as 'a prophetic institution whose purpose is the criticism of sin'. Prophecy means discerning within contemporary events the signs of activity of God. The Biblical criteria of such signs are clear enough. If an event is opening up a greater possibility for the liberation of all peoples, then its agent, whoever that may be, can be called the servant of God's purpose or even the rod of His anger. If people are seen to be clearly offering good news to the poor, liberty to the oppressed, sight to the blind, then they are sharing in the ministry of Jesus Christ. If the nations are feeding the hungry, nurturing the prisoner, caring for the homeless, then they are called the blessed of the Father. Wherever these things are happening, even to the least of God's people, He is there among them and His Church should celebrate the sign and name the name of the Lord even though so often His work is anonymous and He remains incognito.

This naming the name of the Lord is one of the most important evangelistic tasks of the Church. The trouble is that so often Christians seem eager to name that name within the confines of the Church itself but fail to recognise the face when they meet Him within the world. When we do name the name of Jesus among those who are actually doing the works He did, we may find ourselves in strange company, but our message will carry greater credibility. It was at a crowded conference at the Roundhouse, made up of young people committed to the campaign against world hunger, that Archbishop Helder Camara of Brazil won a standing ovation when he said, 'I don't care what you call yourselves. If you are standing alongside the poor and the hungry of this world, you are standing alongside Jesus Christ.' Because they knew that that was where the Archbishop himself was standing, they could hear what he was saying when he named his Lord. It was at a Women's Rights rally with women who had long since written off the Church as the last bastion of male privilege, buttressed by theological prejudice, that serious attention was given to Una Kroll's public confession of Jesus as the great liberator of women. It was standing in the streets of Willesden alongside the exploited Asian women workers at the Grunwick factory that David Haslam gave the most effective expression of both his pastoral and his political role as the local minister of a Church committed to proclaim in the highways and byways a Kingdom which comes as promise to the oppressed and as a judgement to the oppressor.

Just as important, where the works of Christ are flagrantly being contradicted, then the Church's role is to expose evil and to name the sin. If people are to repent, to think again, and to believe the gospel, they have to be reminded of the things that need rethinking in the light of the good news of God's love for all the world. It is not enough to denounce sin in general, nor even to attack private sin in particular. One role of the Church is to be involved in unmasking and exposing the unjust structures of the world we live in in order to encourage Christians to share in the liberating process.

This is what the World Council of Churches has attempted to do in recent years through its Programme to Combat Racism. This programme has come under fire in Britain not because it so clearly denounces racism as a sin. Almost every Church would agree with that denunciation and most of the Church leaders in Britain have signed strong resolutions expressing their abhorrence of the evils of racism. What has upset people has been the exposure of the whole anatomy of racial oppression and the ways in which we in Britain feed off its profits in the preservation of our own privileges. When British oil companies were exposed, for example, as flagrantly violating international sanctions against the illegal racist regime in Rhodesia and thereby fuelling the military power of Ian Smith's forces, British Churches, many of whom were shareholders in those companies, were put under a clear moral obligation to make public protest. Yet in the debate surrounding this shareholder action, some Church financiers spoke as though they almost wished no one had revealed the truth in the first place. Embarrassment over their own complicity with the powers of oppression has however in no way inhibited the British Churches from criticism of the World Council's stance of solidarity with the oppressed, precisely on the grounds that this might appear to suggest complicity in violence. In the fierce controversy erupting out of the whole Programme to Combat Racism people have been compelled to do some rethinking, not only of what they hear mainly through the channels of propaganda but also of what they sift through the mesh of their own prejudices, an educational process which has in some cases led to the change of heart necessary to open up the gospel possibility of a radical change of commitment.

The invitation to believe in that gospel and to become committed to its outworking follows the proclamation of the Kingdom and the call to repentance. Biblical theology views all history since the coming of Jesus as a new regime. The Church must constantly therefore be confronting people with a crisis of choice. Do they go on living under the old dispensation of the powers, or do they obey the new authority of the Kingdom? People of faith should be enabled to live in this world as those who have hope in a new future. The Church should become the place where this hope is celebrated in liturgies which take on the literal meaning of that word as they express the work and energy of the people in giving substance to their hopes and in being committed to the shaping of a radically new future.

So the liturgy becomes itself a part of the Church's proclamation of the revolution inaugurated by the Kingdom. Many of the hymns the Church sings celebrate the liberation. The advent cry to Immanuel to come to the rescue of captive Israel is no mere figure of speech. It is a recalling of that Exodus story which has become the motif of the freedom movements of all time. The Magnificat shockingly celebrates the social upheaval in which the values of the established order of society are stood on their head. The hymns of the early Church recall the martyrs who pitted their strength against the powers and refused to be dominated by them. Slaves sang the freedom songs of Jesus and abolitionists wrote hymns hailing the Lord's anointed who came to break oppression. Today the freedom and folk movements sing their songs too which surprisingly find their way into some of the most conservative churches. Singing the Lord's song in a strange land can in itself raise a political awareness and strengthen a commitment to change. The problem for many of us in Britain is that we sing the Lord's song but we often fail to recognise how strange the land is!

Faith moves through prayer to politics. The congregation which prays in obedience to the Lord that His Kingdom may come on earth should also be prompted to look on all the kingdoms of this earth as the Kingdom which belongs rightfully to God, to be measured by the plumbline of His justice and to be subject to the scrutiny of His mercy. In that sense all intercession for the nations becomes political.

It was amusing to hear recently a Member of Parliament complaining on radio about what he called the political content of the intercessions his young curate had been leading in Church. 'He actually prayed for Mozambique and Angola, drawing the congregation's attention (and presumably the Almighty's) to what he called the enormous task of reconstruction being undertaken by the new governments of those countries!' he protested. 'Do you then regard all prayer for governments as political propaganda?' asked the interviewer. 'Would you omit prayers even for our own queen and all in authority under her?' 'Of course not,' responded the MP. 'I'm simply complaining about these left-wing propagandists.' Presumably he believed that only prayer for right-wing regimes was acceptable in the heavenly regions, a political assessment if ever there was one!

The link between liturgy and politics became very clear at a recent formal service of consecration of a deacon, held in the context of a High Church tradition in a South London church, and appropriately called a Celebration of Freedom. The congregation was a multiracial gathering of people committed to the cause of racial justice; the celebrants were the exiled Bishop of Namibia, the Barbadian vicar of the parish and the African deacon who was being commissioned to go as chaplain to the SWAPO forces. The liturgy was the ancient liturgy of the Church with the prayers for mercy and peace being presented with incense before the throne of the Eternal God. Worship in this dimension strengthens the participants for the immediate struggles of the present moment as it sets their hearts and minds upon the eschatological, invincible hope of an eternal Kingdom. It is this combination of contemplation and action which gives living reality to traditional acts of worship.

At the other end of the ecclesiastical spectrum, it is increasingly evident that Pentecostal groups expressing in spontaneous, energetic worship their affirmation of the Power of the Spirit and their confidence in the Lord's providential care are becoming an empowering force in the life of many black communities in Britain. Having asserted in worship their assurance of their place in the Kingdom of God, they rightly resist in their daily lives any attempt to turn them into second-class citizens of the United Kingdom, or to devalue as being of less worth those bought with so high a price as the blood of Christ. A recent television documentary entitled 'Gospel Heroes' showed one such group going straight from their prayer meetings into programmes of direct community action and self-help projects.

The revolution does not only need to be announced. It has to be enacted. Ask anyone in Cuba to demonstrate what the revolution means and you will be taken to see the astonishing achievement of an agricultural cooperative, the impressive new methods in psychiatric treatment, the nationwide health services and educational systems, all demonstrating what is being done under the auspices of the new regime.

What would be the equivalent demonstration of the effects of the Christian revolution? 'The Church,' wrote Karl Barth, 'is God's provisional demonstration of His intention for all humanity.' Such a concept provides a somewhat devastating criterion to apply to the notices of any church's weekly activities. Those whose theology is of a God who makes all things new and of a Christ who came to set people free might well ask of the weekly notices what part each of these particular activities plays in the renewing, liberating process. Even to take a local newspaper and compare the headlines which may well reflect the major concerns of that community with the paragraphs reporting on the current programmes of local churches can be a depressing exercise, in that it often reveals not so much the sublime indifference of those whose minds are set upon heaven but the absurd irrelevance of so much of what is going on on earth.

Some would assert that the Church's political and social responsibility is most evidently exercised through individual Christians who take their faith personally into the arena of political and community action or try to work out the implications of their faith within all the complexities of daily working life. Yet such activity is still often regarded as extra to the normal routine of Church life and those who are most immersed in it often confess that they feel isolated and unsupported by the mainstream of Church activity. One demonstration of the seriousness with which the Church takes society would be the giving of greater priority to those Lay Training Centres and Institutes of Church and Society where lay men and women working out their Christian commitment in this way are enabled to share their insights and to feel sustained by the whole Christian community. Sadly, lay training is often the first programme to be cut on a strained Church budget and even foundations such as the William Temple College are regarded as somewhat exotic 'extra-mural' activities and are imperilled by lack of sufficient resources.

Equally important in the overall strategy of the Church's mission are those action groups which reconnoitre through research or engage in practical attack on that which militates against God's reign of justice and love. Groups like Christian Action, with its commitment to the defence and aid of the oppressed, or Christians Against Racism and Fascism, determined to challenge in Christ's name the racist nature of British society, or the Fellowship of Reconciliation, taking seriously non-violent action for peace and campaigning against the arms trade, all these should be seen as the Church's 'shock-troops' opening up the way for the whole Christian community to move in on new areas of protest and positive action.

Another clear voice of Christian witness in the contemporary world is

that of Christian publications which are concerned primarily to engage in
a serious critique of society and to encourage the kind of counter-
consciousness Christians need if they are to withstand the massive
pressures of modern propaganda. Yet periodicals like *Christian Statesman,*
with its serious theological commentary on contemporary events, or even
the World Council of Churches' publication *One World,* with its wide
international coverage, have minimal circulation within the Churches in
Britain.

What of the corporate commitment of the Churches to action for social
change? There was a time about a decade ago when churches in Britain
seemed eager to adopt new agendas for their programmes of action within
the community. *The People Next Door* course of study led to a new
Agenda for the Churches, listing the many calls for service that would be
made upon any congregation that took its mission to the local community
really seriously. A whole new concept of what might be called *diakonia*
became acceptable. Many churches put their premises at the disposal of
the community in new ways. Play groups and day centres, advice bureaux
and Samaritan services — all these came increasingly to be regarded as
legitimate activities for churches to be engaged in as they became 'health
centres' in the fullest sense of that word. Yet laudable as all these activities
are, not many of them were directed at the much more difficult job of
trying to change the very structures of the society that cause the kinds of
need these voluntary services were designed to meet. Indeed, the social
service given by the Church can sometimes unwittingly merely seem to
sanctify the present exploitative political and economic order, binding up
the wounds of the victims but not doing enough to catch the thieves!

But it is very difficult to get a local congregation to realise this. It is
easy enough, for example, to recruit young people from a suburban area
to go into a down-town neighbourhood and help in the voluntary
redecorating of old people's homes or organising children's play groups.
But fill them in on the story of what causes those bad housing conditions
and that lack of open space, and then try to persuade them to go back
into the suburb and begin campaigning for a more equitable expenditure
on housing, or for more open space in the inner city area, and you are
likely to run into real resistance from suburban congregations who do not
wish to risk that kind of confrontation. Sometimes the philosophy of the
Church seems to be that aid is good so long as it does not actually change
anything at either local or international level.

There was a time when it was argued that it was doctrine that divided
the Churches whilst the *diakonia* united them. But we have seen in recent
years that when that *diakonia* takes the form of action for radical change,
such as the Programme to Combat Racism or the Christian Parity Group
or the demands for a New International Economic Order, then the

Churches are as much in danger of becoming divided over these issues as they once were over doctrine.

Yet there is emerging today from right across the life of the Churches an understanding of ecumenism which leads not only to the search for Church unity but also, as essential to that, the commitment to the unity of all humanity. M M Thomas, the former Moderator of the World Council of Churches, once described the Church as 'the guardian and spokesman of this Utopian vision, the hope of the historical possibility of a new humanity liberated from oppression'. The basic issue for the Churches today is how far this vision, and action towards the realisation of it, can be incorporated within the very community of the Church itself and how far there can be held together within the community, the *koinonia,* those who see the Church's task as primarily one of charity and reconciliation and those who see it rather in terms of solidarity and the struggle for that justice without which there can be no peace. As M M Thomas went on to say, 'How can we be both messengers of peace in a world of strife and messengers of strife in a world of false peace?'

Yet the reality of the Church community is that it is even more deeply divided than most other human institutions. Not only is it undermined by the great chasms of discrimination which disrupt the foundation of all human societies, the divisions of race and class and sex, but it is also surrounded with walls of ecclesiastical division, buttressed by centuries of prejudice which still stand relatively unshaken by the battering rams of ecumenical enthusiasts.

'We have learned that divided Churches cost lives,' said Gordon Gray of Northern Ireland, reporting on the situation in his country to the World Council of Churches' Fifth Assembly. He reminded us that this was not because the Irish conflict could accurately be described as a religious war, but because any divisions among people, particularly those that are religiously nurtured, become the festering points of a social and political poison which ultimately destroys the whole body.

The failure to overcome even the ecclesiastical divisions enfeebles the witness of the whole Christian community. But, even more, the fact that the Church among all institutions in British society is one of the most clearly identifiable in terms of class, most nearly separated on the basis of race and most deeply defensive of discrimination by sex makes nonsense of its claim to prefigure a new humanity. It is therefore within its own common life, its own *koinonia,* that the most radical change of all needs to be made if the Church is to be able, with any credibility, to fulfil its God-given commission of announcing that the Kingdom of God has come, of enacting His rule among the peoples and of embodying the new order and community which is to be inaugurated for the whole human family.

16. The Class Struggle and Christian Love

Herbert McCabe O.P.

Even the most sympathetic pronouncements by the Christian Churches about political liberation, even the friendliest approaches by Christians towards various kinds of Marxists have a way of ending up with the proviso that Christians can have nothing to do with the idea of an inevitable class struggle. Christians who willingly accept that we now need to dismantle capitalist structures of ownership and control, Christians who are perfectly happy with the prospect of a socialist society, still baulk at the idea of the class struggle as the only possible means to this end.

Now I do not think that this is a contemptible position; I do not think that Christians who adopt it are wicked class enemies secretly in collusion with the bourgeois state, but I think they are wrong and I shall try to show why. If it is true, as I think , that the class struggle *is* the revolution – not just a means towards it, but the thing itself – and if it is true that the Christian gospel of love is incompatible with this, then quite evidently the Christian gospel is incompatible with revolutionary liberation: one of the few positions shared by the International Marxist Group, Mrs Thatcher and Joseph Stalin.

I think this position has a good deal to be said for it, at least at first sight; it is supported by arguments that need to be considered. Christians who rush mindlessly into class confrontations because Jesus wants us to fight a lot of godless capitalists and their lackeys are no more intellectually respectable than Christians who rushed into the Vietnam war because Jesus wants us to fight a lot of godless communists. Nonetheless, if we examine the arguments, they turn out to be mistaken, as I now hope to show.

First of all let us eliminate some fairly simple confusions. One of them arises out of the word 'struggle' itself and a lot of other words that get themselves used in this context: exhortations to 'smash the bourgeois state' or for 'increased militancy' are all violent uses of language so that argument about the class struggle gets mixed up with an argument about violence. People committed to the class struggle are thought to be people especially addicted to trying to solve political and economic problems by violence. Now this is a muddle. There is a Christian argument against the use of violence and there is another Christian argument against participating in the class struggle; both these arguments are, I think, mistaken but they are different arguments because the class struggle and political violence are by no means the same thing.

It is perfectly possible to believe passionately in the importance of the class struggle and to renounce all political violence. It would be perfectly possible for a Christian to hold that the gospel prevents him from ever killing anyone but positively encourages him to subvert and overthrow the ruling class. Further than that: a Christian or a non-christian might well say that political violence is not only different from the class struggle but is actually opposed to it. People who provoke violent confrontations with the ruling class, he might argue, are, wittingly or not, objectively acting as agents of the ruling class. Political violence, he might say, is just romantic adventurism or plain bad temper and is invariably counter-revolutionary. Now I think this too is a very plausible position. You have only to see how the violence of the Provisionals in Northern Ireland has intensified sectarian tensions to realise that this kind of thing is the enemy of real working class unity and militancy. And then there is the general argument that violence is the speciality of the ruling class; they are better at it and better equipped for it; if you meet them on their own ground, in their own terms, playing the game by their rules, they are bound to win. For every idealist gunman you can recruit, they can pay and train a hundred unfortunate young men from the big unemployment pools of the North East or Clydeside. When it comes to the brute primitive business of who can kill most people, the rich are always going to win. General Patton's remark that you do not win wars by dying for your country but by getting the other man to die for *his* country applies with equal force to the class war. As James Connolly put it long ago:

'One great source of the strength of the ruling class has ever been their willingness to kill in defence of their power and privileges. Let their power be once attacked either by foreign foes or by domestic revolutionaries, and at once we see the rulers prepared to kill and kill and kill. The readiness of the ruling class to order killing, the small value the ruling class has ever set upon human life, is in marked contrast to the reluctance of all revolutionaries to shed blood.'

The wealthy and powerful are wealthy and powerful in part because

they are better at killing; the one thing they cannot do is carry on forever
the fiction that their interests coincide with the interests of most of the
community. They cannot forever con people into believing that it is in
their own interests and that of their families to work or to die for the
profit of the ruling class. Any action that helps to expose this fiction, any
action that serves to organise the working class — which is to say almost
everybody in the community — in their *own* interests strikes a really
dangerous blow at the power of our rulers, immensely more dangerous
than any bullet or bomb. Through their newspapers, our rulers evince
proper outrage at the murderous activities of urban terrorists, but on those
rare occasions when the unions show some sign of mild militancy the tone
becomes one of hysterical fear. It may of course be necessary, in order to
expose the great fiction, in order to organise the workers, to do illegal
things (for publicity if for nothing else) but this is a very different matter
from a military confrontation with the state. A totally pacifist Christian
could well advocate illegal action, obstruction and the rest of it, not
because he imagines that such pinpricks will of themselves weaken the
power of the police or the army, but because they are part of a genuine
subversive plan to organise the power of the people.

In any case what is illegal and what is legal is a relative and shifting
thing. Any activity that begins to pose a genuine threat to the capitalist
order will in the course of time be made illegal — think of the current
move to 'tighten the law' on picketing. And of course now that, with the
Prevention of Terrorism Act, Britain has become a police state, it is no
longer necessary even to accuse a person of an illegal act before taking
him or her into custody. The Act has, naturally, nothing at all to do with
the prevention of terrorism; of the thousands who have now been arrested
and detained under it, the enormous majority had absolutely nothing to
do with terrorism and could not be charged with so much as a parking
offence — though one man they picked up and imprisoned was charged
with 'wasting police time'. The Act exists to make it easier to harass and
persecute people who show signs of being a nuisance to the capitalist
order. I mention this merely to indicate the wide and inevitably increasing
area of non-violent illegal actions (not to mention the perfectly legal
actions for which you can now be detained) that a Christian pacifist might
find necessary as part of the non-violent class struggle. There is no
substance at all to the belief that such a pacifist must logically confine his
actions to those that are still sanctioned by the law.

I have spoken at some length about this version of the Christian
challenge to our society — that of the person who is actively committed
to the class struggle and perfectly prepared to do things that will land him
or her in jail, but who is wholly opposed to violence — firstly because it is
a fairly common one amongst Christians; and secondly because it needs to

answer and usually fails to answer an objection from the point of view of the gospel; and thirdly because I think it is mistaken, though not at the moment very *importantly* mistaken.

Last things first: I think Christian pacifists are mistaken in ruling out violence in all circumstances, for the very conventional reason that in the end the ruling class will always protect its interests with gunfire, as we have seen it doing in Chile and throughout Latin America in recent years. In the end the workers will need not only solidarity and class consciousness but guns as well; but in this country, and in the Western world as a whole, this moment has not yet arrived; the capitalist class has by no means yet dismantled the apparatus of democracy; a certain freedom of communication, certain civil rights, despite all harassment of militants, make the class struggle a good deal easier to organise here than in many countries. While this situation obtains, our job is peaceful and efficient organisation, education and propaganda. Any adventurist violent posturings, which will merely hasten the dismantling of these democratic freedoms, are simply counter-revolutionary. That is why Christian pacifists are not *at the moment* very importantly mistaken; for the moment violence is not on the revolutionary agenda in this country. Their pacifism may, indeed, cause such Christians mistakenly to deplore *necessary* violence in other parts of the world, but this too doesn't matter much because the fighting men and women of Zimbabwe, Iran or Nicaragua can generally survive being deplored by rather distant Christians.

I think, then, that the pacifist is mistaken in supposing that violence is always incompatible with the Christian demand that we love our neighbour, and later I shall explain why I think this, but I also think that he is vulnerable from, so to speak, the other end. As I have said, he needs to answer a further objection from the point of view of the gospel: the objection that the class struggle *itself,* whether violent or not, and if non-violent, whether illegal or not, and if not illegal, whether landing you in the hands of the Special Branch or not, is an unchristian and deplorable thing.

In this matter I propose to come to the aid and comfort of the hypothetical Christian pacifist militant. I propose to try and show that participation in the class struggle is not only compatible with Christian love but is demanded by it; then I want to go on from there to my other point at which I shall try to show that there are circumstances in which even violence itself — by which I mean killing people — is not only compatible with Christian love but demanded by it; though these circumstances, as I have said, do not at present obtain in the Western capitalist world.

'Blessed are the meek for they shall inherit the earth.

'Blessed are the peacemakers for they shall be called sons of God.'

'I say to you: do not resist one who is evil. But if anyone strikes you on the right cheek, turn to him the other also.
'You have heard that it was said: "You shall love your neighbour and hate your enemy." But I say to you: Love your enemies and pray for those that persecute you.
'I say to you: Everyone who is angry with his brother shall be liable to judgement; whoever insults his brother shall be liable to the Council, whoever says "You fool" shall be liable to the Gehenna of fire.'

These are familiar but powerful passages from the Sermon on the Mount.

'Peter said to Jesus: "Lord, how often shall my brother sin against me and I forgive him? As many as seven times?" Jesus said to him: "I do not say to you seven times, but seventy times seven times." '

That's again from Matthew. But of course the thing isn't confined to Matthew. The command to love your neighbour as yourself is already in Galatians and in Mark. Luke as well has the passage about loving your enemies. John is slightly different; he speaks more of love than any other New Testament writer but I think it might be argued that for him this means primarily solidarity amongst the comrades of the Christian movement. He does not, at least directly, speak of loving all men, but he does speak of 'the brother, as in I *John* 4.20: 'He who does not love his brother whom he has seen cannot love God whom he has not seen.'
So all in all it cannot be denied that if the Christian gospel is about anything it is about people loving each other. It is not, as is sometimes thought, *simply* about this: on the contrary it is first of all about God loving us, but the sign that we recognise this love of God for us, the sign of our faith, is that we love each other. And if we have any doubts about what the early Church thought that love implied, we should look at I *Corinthians:* 'Love is patient and kind ... it is not arrogant ... Love does not insist on its own way, love endures all things...'
Now it certainly looks as if you cannot preach the absolute necessity of love (which does not insist on its own interests, which endures all things) and at the same time preach that people should fight for their rights, should refuse to endure their working conditions. Can the struggle against the transnationals or the SAS be carried on *meekly*? If the peacemakers are blessed then it must always be better to avoid a strike or any kind of confrontation – and so on.
Clearsighted parsons and bishops right through the eighteenth and nineteenth centuries have for the most part surely understood this: the

Church must be against social conflict, against the agitator, the revolutionary. 'Hell is not hot enough nor eternity long enough to punish the leaders of the Fenians' as the celebrated bishop intoned. Equally clearsighted agitators and revolutionaries have been of the same opinion during the same period. The Church is inextricably bound up with the class enemy, is she not? She must and will support the *status quo* and the powers that be. There will no doubt be occasional quarrels between Church and capitalist state when their interests conflict, just as there will be occasional quarrels between capitalist states themselves, there will be anti-clerical persecutions just as there will be national wars, but basically the Church and the bourgeoisie are on the same side against the working class. The gospel of love can *safely* be preached to the bourgeoisie, for to them it will just mean philanthropy and soup for the deserving poor; it can *profitably* be preached to the workers for it will emasculate their struggle and induce them to bear their fate with Christian resignation.

All this was nice and simple, though even in the eighteenth and nineteenth centuries there were a fair number of people — a lot of them Methodists, but also Roman Catholics and High Anglicans and others — to point out that the gospel and the interests of the Church are not precisely synonymous. Nevertheless it was fairly simple. It is only in our present age that the facts of history have begun to be unkind to this simple view. The daily news from Latin America shows Christians as posing a far greater threat to business interests than communist parties ever did. In Africa the challenge to colonialism and white racism does not come substantially from strict Marxist theorists but from good Catholics like Nyerere and Mugabe, and good Protestants like Kaunda and Nkomo — not by any means from *all* Christians, I need hardly say, but from a sufficiently substantial number of them to worry both the police and the old-fashioned theorists. Are all these just confused and contradictory — Castro when he speaks respectfully of the revolutionary role of the Church in Latin America, or the Christians who play an active part in Marxist movements — are they all hopelessly muddled, or do we have to make some important modifications to the theory? Let us look and see.

First of all, so that we shall not be altogether at cross purposes, a word about what the class struggle *is*. This will have to be a very simplified, even an over-simplified, word, but I want to be as brief as possible. The class struggle is not, in the first place, a struggle between the haves and the have nots. It has very little to do with what people in England call 'class distinctions', meaning a peculiarly English kind of snobbery. It is not differences of wealth that cause class differences, but class differences that cause differences of wealth. The worker by his labour creates a certain amount of wealth, only part of which is returned to him in the form of wages, etc. The rest is appropriated by the employer, or capitalist, so called because his function is to accumulate capital in this way. The capitalist receives from a great many workers the extra wealth which they produce but do not need for their subsistence and minimal contentment, and bringing all this wealth together he is able to invest, to provide the conditions under which more work may be done – and so on. On this fundamental division between worker and employer the whole class system rests. The worker is whoever by productive work actually creates wealth. The employer is not simply anyone who makes overall decisions about what work shall be done and how; he is the one who takes the surplus wealth created by the worker and uses it (in his own interests of course) as capital. Capitalism is just the system in which capital is accumulated for investment, in their own interests, by a group of people who own the means of production and employ large numbers of other people who do not own the means of production but produce both the wealth which they receive back in wages and the surplus wealth which is used for investment by the owners.

There is of course nothing wrong with the accumulation of capital. If all the wealth created by the worker were retained by him for consumption there would be no development of new techniques, no human progress in production, no creation of civilisation. It is possible to imagine, and I think there have actually existed, societies in which hardly any such progress has taken place because either there was very little surplus value created by the primitive work that was done – hardly more than was enough for the subsistence of the worker and his family – or else the surplus was simply consumed by the rich or used for military purposes without being put to productive use as capital. Such societies might be quite stable, they would contain rich and poor families (the rich being those strong enough to keep the others in subjection) but it would not strictly contain any classes. Feudal, aristocratic, pre-capitalist society can be at least schematically represented in this way. The feudal landlord and his family, like a Mafia Godfather, is strong enough both to keep his tenants, peasants and serfs in subjection and in return to protect them from arbitrary attack, robbery and disaster from outside. If you happen to think that it is in some way wrong or unjust that some people should be rich and have an easy life while others should be poor and have a hard life, then you will probably think such a society unjust. But as a matter of fact most people living in such societies do not seem, so far as we know, to have felt this way except when conditions for the poor became exceptionally bad. They just took it for granted that there would be the rich man in his castle and the poor man at the gate, and in a highly unstable world the rich man did provide minimal protection, law and order; he had the military power to subdue gangsters and casual predators. When you felt resentful of the rich there was always the gospel to assure you that he was probably corrupted by his wealth and due for eternal damnation; but there was nothing in the gospel (and there still is nothing in the gospel) to say that everyone has to have equal shares of wealth; there is plenty to tell you not to be preoccupied with such questions. Of course there was a great deal of injustice in such feudal society, arbitrary rapine and cruelty, the greed of the lord grabbing more than his customary dues from his subjects, and so on, and there was plenty in the gospel and the traditional teachings of the Church to condemn this, but nothing to suggest anything especially diabolical about the existence of rich and poor.

Under such a feudal set-up the rich man is one who lives more luxuriously than others; a capitalist is quite a different matter. He is not, except maybe incidentally, a rich man living in luxury; he is a man whose function it is to accumulate capital and invest it. He has no slaves or serfs to keep in subjection and correspondingly no job of protecting anyone. There are no customary dues, no recognised rights and obligations, no privileges, no servility. There emerges what Marx calls 'civil society'. Theoretically at any rate everyone is free, they are only bound by the contract they enter into. The worker has something to sell as dearly as possible, his labour, and the capitalist wants to buy it as cheaply as possible so as to have the maximum left over for capital investment. In this matter their interests fundamentally conflict. In our schematic feudal set-up, you could say that each person has his or her niche in the system, even though some niches were much more comfortable than others. There was a roughly coherent static pattern of social relationships and it was felt to be an important task to preserve this stasis and to minimise conflict within it. Ideally at any rate, nobody has a niche under capitalism; capitalism is not a system, it is a process. It is a process of struggle, of competition — competition between rival capitalist which leads to greater efficiency but also leads to military struggle between the nation states created by capitalism; hence the national wars which by their consumption of armaments are in themselves an important element in the later capitalist economy. Competition even more fundamentally between the capitalist and the ultimate source of all economic value, the workers who under capitalism become a class distinguished by the fact that all they have to sell is their labour which they have to sell in the best market available. For a variety of reasons and in a variety of aspects this capitalist process is unstable. I don't want to go here into complex economic matters which are in any case in dispute amongst Marxists, concerning the inevitable falling rate of profit, the boom/depression cycle and the rest of it; for one thing it is a field in which I fear to tread, but I do want to note one fairly simple and essential instability in the whole process. Capitalism, through industrialisation, creates the conditions for the emergence of an organised working class — large numbers of people who have in common at least an opposing interest to that of the capitalist are brought together to work in the same buildings and live in the same streets. This means that the capitalist inevitably strengthens the hand of his opponents in the capitalist game itself. Capitalism, moreover, by its destruction of feudal privileges and the customary powers of the aristocracy, by bringing the bourgeoisie to power creates the democratic liberties, the relatively free media of communication, the principle of equality before the law and so on within which the organised working class can come to greater political power. When this power becomes too threatening there is a tendency for capitalism to regress from bourgeois democracy to feudal style politics of the kind we call fascism, but this is itself a sign of the instability of the process. Fascism is, roughly speaking, the combination of capitalist economics with feudal politics.

The central point I wish to make throughout this is that the class war is *intrinsic* to capitalism. It is part of the dynamic of the capitalist process itself. It is not as though somebody said: 'Let's have a class struggle, let's adjust the imbalance of wealth by organising the poor workers against the rich capitalists.' Nothing of the kind. The tension and struggle between worker and capitalist is an essential part of the process itself.

Here, however, we have to notice a certain asymmetry in the struggle within capitalism. The capitalist's struggle is simply within the process. The opposite worker's struggle is more than that. It is actually destructive of the process itself. The capitalist method of accumulating capital by the private ownership of the means of production eventually creates the conditions in which it is itself out of date as well as bringing forth the new class which will operate the transition to a new system. The methods and techniques of production developed under capitalism, the interlocking complexities of the industrial process itself, not to mention the complexities of distribution and exchange, mean that control by the free play of the market simply will not work any more. The response to this under capitalism is of course the movement from individual entrepreneur to corporation, from corporation to transnational company and so on. But all this is really only building an appearance of modernity onto an out of date basis which still remains the basis of private, non-social ownership and the market economy. The obvious move is to eliminate the archaic irrelevancy of the market, and with it the archaic irrelevancy of the capitalist class, and to transfer the whole thing to the organised working class. The accumulation of capital and its investment will then not be at the mercy of the maximisation of profit by this or that corporation, but can be organised rationally (and therefore justly) in terms of what people need and want.

As capitalism seeks to readjust itself to the situation it has created, one of its moves is the phasing out, as a significant factor, of the nation state which was originally set up as the protector of local capitalist enterprises. The setting up of the EEC (and for that matter the American civil war which established the first modern common market) is just such a move against the nationalism of early capitalism. To seek to institute social ownership of the means of production while retaining the old nation state — to see 'nationalisation' as a genuine alternative to capitalism — would seem to be a blind alley; the result is merely, as in Russia, the replacement of the capitalist class by a bureaucracy. Nationalisation *within* capitalism, as in Britain, for example, is simply a way of providing at public expense the infrastructure required by national or international capital which cannot be provided at a profit — there is nothing more essentially socialist about a state-run coalmine than there is about a state-run army. It is only in the context of workers' control that nationalisation is socialist.

The struggle of the working class is not, therefore, simply a struggle within capitalism, as though it were a matter of reversing positions and 'putting the workers on top' (as in the game of parliamentary elections); it is a struggle within capitalism which, insofar as it is successful, leads beyond capitalism. As Marx puts it:

'An oppressed class is a vital ingredient of every society based on class antagonism. The emancipation of the oppressed class therefore necessarily involves the creation of a new society... Does this mean the downfall of the old society will be followed by a new class domination expressing itself in a new political power? No, the condition for the emancipation of the working class is the abolition of all classes.'

If the kind of account I have been giving is more or less right, and you don't have to be much of a Marxist to see it as a fairly plausible view of things, then there are certain things we can say:

1. The class struggle is not a product of the envy of the poor for the rich; it is not about establishing some ideal equality between people's incomes.

2. The class struggle is not something we are in a position to *start;* it is a condition of the process called capitalism within which we find ourselves. If anybody could be said to have 'started' the class struggle it was, I suppose, those enterprising medieval men who found ways to get round or break out of the stifling customs and traditions of feudalism and thus found ways to make products available more cheaply and more profitably.

3. The class struggle is not something we are in a position to refrain from. It is just there; we are either on one side or the other. What looks like neutrality is simply a collusion with the class in power.

Now of course everything would be so much simpler if the class struggle were altogether perspicuous, but it is not; it comes in a variety of disguises. In the first place the simple division into two classes won't do. The basic antagonism that lies at the root of society produces a whole series of mutually hostile groupings engaged in shifting alliances and confrontations. It is almost never a simple matter to decide in the case of any particular dispute which side is to be supported in the furtherance of the emancipation of the working class and the consequent abolition of all class antagonisms. Very familiar instances of these difficulties occur with national liberation movements which are always a confusion of different elements struggling for different and sometimes incompatible aims.

Nothing in Karl Marx that I know of and certainly nothing in the New Testament provides you with a simple key to what to do in such cases. Marx said: 'All the struggles within the State, the struggle between democracy, aristocracy and monarchy, the struggle for the franchise, etc, are merely the illusory forms in which the real struggles of the different classes with each other are fought out.' No doubt, but getting through the illusions to the reality is a difficult and delicate business.

What is wrong with capitalism, then, is not that it involves some people being richer than I am. I cannot see the slightest objection to other people being richer than I am; I have no urge to be as rich as everybody else, and no Christian (and indeed no grown-up person) could possibly devote his life to trying to be as rich or richer than others. There are indeed people, very large numbers of people, who are obscenely poor, starving, diseased, illiterate, and it is quite obviously unjust and unreasonable that they should be left in this state while other people or other nations live in luxury; but this has nothing specially to do with capitalism, even though we will never now be able to alter that situation until capitalism has been abolished. You find exactly the same conditions in, say, slave societies and, moreover, capitalism, during its prosperous boom phases, is quite capable of relieving distress at least in fully industrialised societies — this is what the 'Welfare State' is all about. What is wrong with capitalism is simply that it is based on human antagonism, and it is precisely here that it comes in conflict with Christianity. Capitalism is a state of war, but not just a state of war between equivalent forces; it involves a war between those who believe in and prosecute war as a way of life, as an economy, and those who do not. The permanent capitalist state of war erupts every now and then into a major killing war, but its so-called peacetime is just war carried on by other means. The recent strategic arms *limitation* talks (SALT II) have produced an agreement whereby the US should deploy a capacity to inflict 600,000 Hiroshimas on the human race. But at the heart of all this violence is the class war.

It is of course not in the least surprising that those whose whole way of life demands the class war should be the ones to deny its importance or even its existence. For the propagandists of capital, the class war is something invented or instigated by revolutionaries and socialists; in fact it is merely uncovered by them. We are all by now thoroughly familiar with the 'peace-keeping role' of Russian tanks or American bombers or British paratroopers; all such major terrorists proclaim that they are simply maintaining or restoring a peace that has been wantonly shattered by wicked subversives. In exactly the same way the capitalist press and the BBC speak of strikes as disturbances of industrial peace, so that the end of a strike, whatever its outcome, is described as a return to normality and order. There is no reason to take any of these people seriously.

Christianity is deeply subversive of capitalism precisely because it announces the improbable possibility that men might live together without war; neither by domination nor by antagonism but by unity in love. It announces this, of course, primarily as a future and nearly miraculous possibility and certainly not as an established fact; Christians are not under the illusion that mankind is sinless or that sin is easily overcome, but they believe that it will be overcome. It was for this reason that Jesus was executed – as a political threat. Not because he was a political activist; he was not. Although amongst his disciples he attracted some of the Jewish nationalist Zealots, the Provos of the time, they did not attract him. Certainly Jesus was not any kind of socialist – how could anyone be a socialist before capitalism had come into existence? But he was nonetheless executed as a political threat because the gospel he preached – that the Father loves us and therefore, in spite of all the evidence to the contrary, we are able to love one another and stake the meaning of our lives on this – cut at the root of the antagonistic society in which he still lives.

Christianity is not an ideal theory, it is a praxis, a particular kind of practical challenge to the world. Christians, therefore, do not, or should not, stand around saying 'What a pity there is capitalism and the class war'. They say, or should say, 'How are we going to change this?' It might have been nice if we had never had capitalism; who can tell what might have happened? Only the most naive mechanist supposes that history has inevitable patterns so that you could predict every stage of it. It is at least theoretically possible that there might never have been capitalism and that *might* have been nice, though it is hard to see how we could have gone through the enormous strides towards human liberation that were in fact made under and through capitalism. The point is that all that is useless speculation; we do have capitalism, we do have class war; and the Christian job is to deal with these facts about our world.

It is useful to reflect from time to time on the fact that capitalism is, in part, the fruit of Christianity. It was the Christian movement, with its doctrine of the autonomy of the world and its attack on the gods, that made possible the rise of scientific rationalism. There is a direct connection between the doctrine of creation and the presuppositions of scientific explanation. It was the Christian movement that broke the power of the great feudal families, and so on. The Christian movement shattered itself at the Reformation by its involvement in the capitalist revolution. It is only now, with the end of the capitalist era, that those wounds are being healed – now that they are irrelevant. We must expect the involvement of Christians in the socialist revolution to be no less traumatic for the Churches.

There are, as it seems to me, only two available attitudes in the face of the class war: you can either try to go back to a time before it started, you can wish that capitalism had never occurred (and you can imagine you are engaged in building a non-capitalist, non-antagonistic world), or else, faced with the fact of the class war, you can try to win it. The first of these attitudes has too often been adopted by Christians faced with capitalism. They construct an imaginary ideal Christian social order in which class antagonisms will not exist because everybody will love everyone – whereas, of course, people will only in any practical sense love each other when class antagonisms have ceased. If, for example, you look at the papal social teaching from the time of Leo XIII until Vatican II or, to take a more parochial example, if you look at William Temple and the Christian social movement, you will find just such a prescription for an ideal consensus society, a utopian form of socialism or a utopian form of distributism, to which there are two serious objections. The first is that there is no attempt to show how such a society might be brought about in the present stage of history, and the second is that by diverting attention from the realities of the class war such dreaming plays into the hands of one of the protagonists of that war – the one that is on the side of war. It is just as with the Peace Movement in Northern Ireland which began so splendidly as a cry of outrage against sectarian murder but which, precisely because it simply dreamt of peace without offering a programme to achieve it, ended up simply as an instrument of British propaganda. The Peace Women had no more conscious desire to aid and abet British imperialism than Archbishop Temple had to aid and abet the CBI, yet he ended up a couple of years ago being republished with a preface by Edward Heath. That kind of Christian utopianism that finds its home so often in the Liberal or Labour Party is in fact unwittingly, but objectively, reactionary. The only way to end the class war is to win it.

The Christian who looks for peace and for an end to antagonism has no option but to throw himself wholeheartedly into the struggle against the class enemy; he must be unequivocally on one side and not on the other. As I have said, it is not always perfectly simple to sort out which side is which in the various protean disguises that the class struggle takes, but given that they are sorted out there should be no question but that the Christian is on one side with no hankering after the other. The other side is the enemy. If you doubt this, watch how he behaves: he will seek either to buy you or crush you. The world, as John has Jesus saying, will hate you.

Now *how* will you carry on the fight? There are various pieces of advice that might be given, but I would like here to reiterate some traditional ones. In the first place be meek. Blessed are the meek for they shall inherit the earth; pray for those that persecute you; be a peacemaker; do not insult your enemy or be angry with him. Who, after all, wants a comrade in the struggle who is an arrogant, loudmouthed, aggressive bully? The kind of person who jumps on the revolutionary bandwagon in order to work off his or her bad temper or envy or unresolved conflict with parents does not make a good and reliable comrade. Whatever happened to all those 'revolutionary' students of 1968? What the revolution needs is grown-up people who have caught on to themselves, who have recognised their own infantilisms and to some extent dealt with them — people in fact who have listened to the Sermon on the Mount.

It is a simple piece of right-wing lying that those who carry on the struggle are motivated by pride and greed, envy and aggression. Real revolutionaries are loving, kind, gentle, calm, unprovoked to anger; they don't hit back when someone strikes them, they do not insist on their own way, they endure all things; they are extremely dangerous. It is not the revolution but the capitalist competitive process that is explicitly and unashamedly powered by greed and aggression. The Christian demand for love and peace is precisely what motivates us to take part in the class struggle: but more than that, the gospel of love, and in particular the Sermon on the Mount, provides us with the appropriate revolutionary discipline for effective action.

We still need though to face the question of revolutionary violence. How could that be compatible with the Sermon on the Mount? Well, first of all, in this matter we should not lose our sense of humour. There is something especially ludicrous about Christian churchmen coming round to the belief that violence is wrong. There is probably no sound on earth so bizarre as the noise of clergymen bleating about terrorism and revolutionary violence while their cathedrals are stuffed with regimental flags and monuments to colonial wars. The Christian Church, with minor exceptions, has been solidly on the side of violence for centuries, but normally it has only been the violence of soldiers and policemen. It is only when the poor catch on to violence that it suddenly turns out to be against the gospel.

But despite all this, the Church, since it is after all the Christian Church, has never simply professed itself in favour of the violence of the ruling classes, the violence of the status quo. What it has done is to profess itself on the side of justice and to note, quite rightly, that in our fallen world justice sometimes demands violence. This seems to me to make perfect sense — my only quarrel is with the way that justice has so often turned out to coincide with the interests of the rich. Justice and love can involve coercion and violence because the objects of justice and love are not just individual people but can be whole societies. It is an error (and a bourgeois liberal error at that) to restrict love to the individual I-Thou relationship. There is no warrant for this in the New Testament — it is simply a framework that our society has imposed on our reading of the gospels. If we have love for people not simply in their individuality but also in their involvement in the social structures, if we wish to protect the structures that make human life possible, then we sometimes, in fact quite often, find it necessary to coerce an individual for the sake of the good of the whole. The individual who seeks his or her own apparent interests at the expense of the whole community may have to be stopped, and may have to be stopped quickly. To use violence in such a case is admittedly not a perspicuous manifestation of love (if we were trying to teach someone the meaning of the word 'love' we would hardly point to such examples), but that does not mean that it is a manifestation of lack of love. In our world, before the full coming of the kingdom, love cannot always be perspicuous and obvious. We must not hastily suppose that just because an action would hardly do as a paradigm case of loving that it is therefore opposed to love.

To imagine that we will never come across people who set their own private interests above those of the community and seek them at the community's expense, is not only to fly in the face of the evidence, it is also to deny the possibility of sin. It is to deny a great deal about yourself.

All this has been well understood in the mainstream Christian tradition; it has long been recognised that while *injustice* is intrinsically wrong (so that it makes no sense to claim that the reason why you are committing an injustice — killing, let us say, an innocent person — is in order to achieve justice), *violence,* though an evil and never a perspicuous manifestation of love, is not intrinsically wrong; it does not make the same kind of nonsense to say that you are doing violence in order to achieve justice. As I see it, the old theology of the just war is in essence perfectly sound; this was an attempt to lay down guidelines for deciding when violence is just and when it is unjust. The theology was perfectly sensible and rational but what we have now come to see is that the only just war is the class war, the struggle of the working class against their exploiters. No war is just except in so far as it is part of this struggle.

As I have already said, it seems to me that violence can have very little part in the class struggle as such, but it does seem reasonable to suppose that the ruling class will continually defend its position by violence and it is therefore difficult to see how it could be overthrown in the end without some use of violence. It is not a question of vindictive violence against individuals seen as personally wicked; the revolutionary, who will reject all conspiracy theories of society, is the last person to blame the corrupt social order on the misdeeds of individuals; there is no place for such infantile hatred in the revolution. However difficult it may be to see this, the revolution is for the sake of the exploiter as well as the exploited. Nevertheless it is useless to pretend that there will be no killing of those who defend their injustice by violence. It is even more difficult to see how the early phases of socialism could be protected from reactionary subversion without some form of coercion. The example of Chile stands as an appalling warning of the ruthlessness of capitalism when it sees itself really threatened. I cannot see how such necessary violence and coercion are in any way incompatible with Christian love. Of course they are not perspicuous examples of love, and of course they would have no place in a truly liberated society, and of course no place in the Kingdom; but we have not yet reached this point. It is for this reason that we cannot imagine Jesus taking part in such violence; he was wholly and entirely a perspicuous example of what love means; he was and is the presence of the Kingdom itself; we, however, are only on the road towards it.

But not *just* on the road towards it. Christians believe that the Kingdom is not just in the future; because of Christ's passion and resurrection it is also in a mysterious way present. This presence of the future is what we call grace. This means that a Christian cannot fully accept Chairman Mao's saying that there is, as yet, no brotherhood of man, that it must wait until the establishment of communism. From one point of view this is correct, and like Mao the Christian would want to reject the superficial liberal view of the unity of men regardless of creed or class; indeed the brotherhood of man belongs to the future, the real unity of the human race is a unity in grace, in Christ; but the future itself is not *just* in the future. Christ is not only the Omega point, He also lives in us even now. This means that Christians, in a sense, look at the present from the perspective of the future. This is what makes genuine *forgiveness* possible. Through grace, through the life of Christ in him, the Christian is able, in an odd way, to adopt the perspective of God, who loves both the just and the unjust. This does not make the unjust any less unjust; this does not in any way diminish the need for the struggle, the need for smashing the power of the exploiter and oppressor, but it does, in the end, make hatred impossible. There is a paradox, but no contradiction, in being able by the grace of God to love the person you must fight; there is a paradox, but no contradiction, in having an enemy who must be destroyed and yet who is not in any ultimate sense *the* enemy but one for whom Christ also dies; there is a paradox, but no contradiction, in fact, in loving your enemies. And the paradox lies in God who is not just the future, not just the transcendent towards which we strive, but is Emmanuel, God with us, the future which is already with us, drawing us to Himself.

Postscript

Rex Ambler and David Haslam

It is impossible to attempt a 'summary' of the articles which appear above. This is merely an effort to draw out some of the areas of similarity and of difference among the variety of writers who have contributed and to indicate the themes around which the next 'act' in the drama may need to be constructed. The first theme is the ongoing debate between Christianity and Marxism, which despite the slightly dismissive comments in some of the essays above, still seems alive, well and remarkably creative. The second is related to the writers' views of the Church and the question of whether prophetic witness comes from within or without the ecclesiastical institution, an argument which probably is nearly as old as the Church itself. Thirdly there is the tension between action and reflection and the problem that it seems that only in action do Christians find themselves whipped along the Calvary road. For too many churchgoers the action dimension, especially in political terms, is still to be avoided at all costs.

In the Christian-Marxist debate we are suggesting that, as the terms are currently understood, it is not possible for one to be both, although as a Christian one may well be informed by Marxism and apply it as an invaluable tool. Third World theologians, while warning that their insights cannot be transferred 'en masse' into the Western milieu, state definitively that Christians cannot and must not ignore the analysis and the insights of Marxism for interpreting the present world scene. Bonino has said this explicitly elsewhere and repeats it implicitly here. We cannot distinguish, as so much Western churchmanship tries to do, between the 'public' and the 'private' spheres. Most theologians belong to the academic bourgeoisie, which cannot be expected either to understand the world or to wish to change it. The sounding boards for the composing of a genuine theology, says Bonino, are the poor, the excluded, the oppressed. It is astonishing how often that crucial insight is quoted in Christian circles, and how rarely it is acted upon.

Yeo too makes clear that the ideological inspiration upon which he freely draws is Marxism. It is Marx who accurately predicted the growth, divisiveness and crisis of capitalism, and who points to the ultimate contradiction at the heart of capitalist society, the conflict between capital and labour. The stories too, in their own ways, are all highly critical of capitalist society and the Church's 'syncretism' within it (e.g. Manning). Haslam, Moore and Manning point to the destructiveness of capitalism in its various forms, the amoral ethics of international finance, the possessiveness over buildings and worship of ordinary church people, the encouragement of racism by a system bent on profit and power. The other three stories point to the alternatives, and their difficulties, common ownership of possessions, cooperative principles at work, and the replacement of the aggressive competitiveness which is primarily male, by the sharing and giving which is primarily female.

John Vincent is the one writer distinctly critical of Marxism. He regards it as too inflexible and too dated to be of use as we look to the 'next kind of society' we seek. Furthermore, in practical terms, according to Vincent, Marxists are no more effectively radical than Christians. Vincent separates, in what he refers to as 'Christocentric radicalism', the political and the theological spheres. He puts the case forcibly for this. The case against may be developed around the necessity of a serious political and economic analysis in our doing of theology, of who holds the power in our society and what forces are strong enough to challenge and oppose. Cullinan too takes a critical approach to Marxism, commenting that 'the reduction of radical politics to mere economics' merely exacerbates the 'dullness and boredom' of today. That is undoubtedly as true of some Marxists as it is untrue of others.

Finally, McCabe builds a Marxist world-view so intricately into his theology that it is hard to distinguish one from the other. McCabe's response might be that it would be foolish to try. Its strength is a clear analysis of how things are as they are and theoretically what measures should be taken to change them. Its weakness may be that it does not indicate, or name, the groups, movements, organisations who are to implement the necessary changes. Where are the signs that the Love Revolution is on the move? We hope there are some in this volume; McCabe's opinion of their efficacy would be illuminating. It may not be without interest to note that according to Tony Benn's piece on 'The Levellers', Christianity was spawning Marxist insights, analyses and solutions long before the great man himself was dreamt of.

The second theme revealing both convergence and divergence is that which focuses on whether the prophetic agenda may be either written or decided upon by the Church. To explore this further requires some kind of definition of the Church. Is Father Mario Borelli entirely right, as

Cullinan suggests in his opening anecdote, to state 'I am the Church'? He may well be, but there are other 'churches' which, as Borelli himself must know all too well, will give no assistance to what he is doing and may on occasions actually oppose it. Who is the true Church? Where is the agenda for prophets being written?

If one examines Ken Leech's historical survey, the indications there seem to be that it is only when Christian groups and movements genuinely rub shoulders, engage in debate and ally in activity with similar movements and organisations outside the Church that the real questions are posed and the real agenda items raised. Many so-called Christian socialists allowed their programme to be dictated overmuch by pietistic or 'theological' insights, without a real engagement with non-Christians, from whom so often theological insights seem to proceed. (For example, would CARAF ever have got off the ground in Britain had the Anti-Nazi League and the Campaign Against Racism and Fascism – CARF – not shown the way?) Movements such as the Catholic Crusade seem to have had a genuine relationship with non-Christian fellows, while those initiated by men such as Maurice and Headlam appear to have been more suspicious of such robust company.

This question is not faced up to overtly in either of the contributions on the Church as an Agent of Social Change, though both Cullinan and Webb imply that external forces are important in Christians' agenda-writing. Cullinan refers to the Philippino Bishop who felt the Church would need the experience of fascism to understand the call to Liberation, while Webb restates the missiological point that the Church is merely the agent of God's sending activity, whereas it is in the friction generated by church/beyond-church initiatives such as the Programme to Combat Racism and Christian Action that prophetic agenda issues become clear.

Some of the stories confirm this suggestion. In Bow Mission, the crisis came when power had to be shared with the non-Christians who were doing the caring, serving, witnessing work of the Church – perhaps a little better than the Christians. And it is the wider feminist movement which has inspired, encouraged and to some extent enabled the Christian Parity Group to pursue its aims while all was horror and dismay in the ecclesiastical corridors.

The final theme exposing similarities and differences between our contributions centres on the dialectic between action and reflection. Christians in the West increasingly face the criticism from theologians representing the powerless, either in Western societies or elsewhere, that there is too much talk, too much liturgy, too much prayer even, and not enough hard action to oppose the oppressive forces present both internally and externally in Western capitalist society. This is illustrated by Benn when he describes how offensive bourgeois 'Christian' society found the programme of the Levellers, and how equally offensive it would be found today if we took seriously the modern correlates of their ideas (see section on 'The Levellers and Today'). Bonino takes up the same point when he notes how Jesus had to use the 'offensive' example of leper, Samaritan, prodigal son, when he wanted to drive home the demanding nature of the Gospel.

Examining the record of the 'Christian Left' in the last 30 years, John Kent notes that the characteristic pose of the religious establishment is one of retreat and that ecclesiastical action tends to concentrate on constructing positions on social and political matters which are not too far behind the progressive sections of society, but not too far ahead of the person in the pew. He rejects, however, that religious action which concentrates exclusively on problems 'over there', rather than right here. It is certainly true that there is no excuse for fighting racism in Southern Africa if one is not fighting it in Britain. Nor will society be transformed 'over there' if it is not in process of being transformed here. This call to transform British society, which is the culmination of Kent's article, is precisely the subject of our enterprise.

Most of all of course it is the 'stories' which issue the challenge to action, or praxis, which challenge the primary movement of political theology. The suggested method of such theology, involving recognition of a problem, initiating an active response, challenging, campaigning, followed by discussion, examination, theological reflection and further planning, is at the heart of most of our stories. None of our story-tellers claims to have got it right first time, or second, or third, but in the ongoing process of reflection and action they would claim that, little by little, the Kingdom is revealed. It is the carefully-chosen and theologically-based course of action which both exposes the real nature and identity of the 'principalities and powers', and which sets the actor on the Calvary road. Each one of our story-tellers has experienced some sacrifice, disappointment or rejection for their efforts. Neither Dietrich Bonhoeffer nor Martin Luther King, nor Camilo Torres, nor Jesus himself was destroyed for merely preaching the gospel. They were destroyed for 'doing the gospel', for opposing the 'powers' and expressing love, justice and reconciliation in concrete actions. The discipline of action and reflection is invaluable to those seeking to express the political dimension of their theology. That is clearly one point upon which all our contributors converge.

The confrontation with the 'principalities and powers', which the Christian prophets mentioned above illustrate, i.e. man's greed, aggression, selfishness, ambition, competitiveness and authoritarianism, is not a chosen one but it is an inevitable one. Its inevitability is demonstrated in history by the bloody destruction of Lollards and Levellers and less bloody but no less effective demolition of nineteenth and twentieth century Christian socialists. Whenever Christians set forth the wild, demanding, scandalous truth of the Gospel, in word and deed, they are ignored, ridiculed, opposed and in some cases hammered, quite literally, into the ground. It will be the Christian's aim to transform society without such bitterness and pain but, as McCabe suggests, that hope is likely to be a vain one.

If the 1980s develop, as they have begun, with increasing divisions in Western society in terms of employment, wealth, welfare provision and race, European Christians are going to need a theology which explains how we have reached this situation, analyses the forces involved and both demonstrates how they may be challenged and inspires us to undertake the challenge. To assist in developing such a theology, we shall need help from two directions, the Christians of the Commonwealth — Africa, Asia, the Caribbean — and the Christians of Europe, East and West.

The heart of what we oppose is a refined and developed capitalist system which thrives on division by race and class and is characterised by unemployment, sexism, the oppression of migrant minorities, trivialisation by the media, declining social welfare provision and the increasing concentration of capital in fewer and fewer hands. It is a system which cannot be opposed in Britain alone, because Britain is now tied, economically and politically, into Europe. This 'Europe', however, is little more than half of the whole. There are hundreds of thousands of Christians in the 'Eastern bloc', to whom 'political theology' poses very different kinds of questions but with whom dialogue would undoubtedly be mutually fascinating.

The directions therefore in which such 'political theologising', i.e. the making concrete of the gospel in society, may take us are threefold. Firstly, a deeper analysis, in economic and political terms, of the faults at the heart of our society and the reasons for them, preferably in dialogue with those who can offer Marxist insights. Secondly, a programme of action and reflection which responds to such analysis, which develops the prophetic agenda created in the friction between Gospel and World and which begins to tackle some of the items on that agenda. And lastly, a dialogue with European Christians, from both East and West, which may not only open up the possibilities of a 'Theology for Britain', but launch us on the road to a 'Theology for Europe'. Which seeks not a reconciliation beyond the current divisions of ideology, race and culture, but a new understanding of and commitment to the enormous responsibilities of a wealthy Europe to the millions of hungry, exploited and innocent 'outsiders' who are, according to what the Church says it believes, 'made in the image of God'.

Contributors

Rex Ambler: Lecturer in the Department of Theology at the University of Birmingham; has been active in various political causes in the city of Birmingham.

Tony Benn: Labour politician, Secretary of State for Energy in the last Labour Government; non-conformist upbringing, has a developing interest in a Theology of the Labour Movement.

Jose Miguez Bonino: Well-known Liberation Theologian from Argentina; has written several books on the dialogue between Christianity and Marxism in Latin America; a President of the World Council of Churches.

Roy Crowder: Became an English teacher after education at Wolverhampton Grammar School and St Peter's College, Oxford; a year living with dossers in Liverpool Petrus Community re-educated him; he now lectures at Sheffield Urban Theology Unit in adult education and is involved in local inner-city action groups.

Thomas Cullinan OSB: A Benedictine monk of Ampleforth; one-time member of the Council of Oxfam and also RC Commission for International Justice and Peace; author of *If the Eye be Sound;* now living in a new monastic house near Liverpool.

David Haslam: Methodist Minister in Harlesden, a multiracial community in north-west London; executive member of Christian Concern for Southern Africa, War on Want, the Anti-Apartheid Movement.

Una Kroll: A general practitioner in South London; campaigner for the

ordination of women in the Anglican Church; founder of the Christian
Parity Group.

John Kent: Professor of Theology at Bristol University; a Methodist, he
has written widely on 19th century religious history.

Ken Leech: An Anglican Priest in the East London parish of Bethnal
Green; an active member of the Jubilee Group.

Basil Manning: South African-born former Travelling Secretary of the
University Christian Movement; now working in a Community
Development/Race Relations project in Deptford.

Herbert McCabe OP: Dominican Priest; editor of *New Blackfriars,* the
leading Christian intellectual magazine on the Christian-Marxist
dialogue; author of works on sacramental theology and moral theology;
currently writing a book on Aquinas' philosophy while lecturing at
University College Dublin.

David Moore: Superintendent of Bow Methodist Mission in East London;
ex-Chairman of CHAR, the Campaign for the Homeless and Rootless.

John Vincent: Methodist Theologian; founder of the Sheffield Inner-city
Ecumenical Mission (SICEM); founder and Director of the Urban
Theology Unit, a research and training service for Christians in urban
society.

Pauline Webb: Ex-Vice Moderator of the World Council of Churches;
active spokesperson on many social issues; Methodist.

Stephen Yeo: A social historian teaching at Sussex University; member of
the Christendom Trust and one-time parliamentary candidate for the
Labour Party, currently active in community politics in East Brighton
(Queenspark); author of *Religion and Voluntary Organisations in
Crisis* (Croom Helm, 1976); currently interested in Co-ops, Friendly
Societies, Working Men's Clubs, Building Societies and all other forms
of Working Class Associations between 1850 and 1950.